YOU
CAN
MOVE
THE
CHEESE!

The Role of an Effective Servant-Leader

STEPHEN PROSSER

Paulist Press
New York/Mahwah, NJ

Cover design by Joy Taylor
Book design by Lynn Else

Library of Congress Cataloging-in-Publication Data

Prosser, Stephen.
    You can move the cheese! : the role of an effective servant-leader /Stephen Prosser.
        p. cm.
    Includes bibliographical references.
    ISBN 978-0-8091-4640-6 (alk. paper)
    1. Leadership. 2. Servant leadership. I. Title.
    HM1261.P76 2010
    658.4′092—dc22

                                                                    2009041058

Published by Paulist Press
997 Macarthur Boulevard
Mahwah, New Jersey 07430

www.paulistpress.com

Printed and bound in the
United States of America

Contents

Acknowledgements and Dedication

Anyone who has written a book will know that for every moment of elation, those times of triumph when you think you have written something acceptable (occasionally profound), there are far more moments when the going gets really tough. The only reason you continue to write is based on sheer willpower—you may even be tempted to throw the manuscript into the proverbial bin by pressing the delete key—and it is during these times that your friends have a valuable part to play: you are grateful for their compliments about previous work and, most of all, for their encouragement to keep on writing.

I have been blessed with many such friends. Some have read the manuscript and made many excellent comments on how things could be improved (reading an early draft of over sixty thousand words is hard work); others have contributed suggestions surrounding principles; and some have been there as a source of encouragement; and some have supplied all three functions. I thank them all, and this book is dedicated to: George Craig, Christine Davies, Tim Pidsley, Andrew Price, Simon Thane, Christopher Ward, Michael Wheatley and, above all, my wife, Lesley, without whose love and support none of this would have been possible.

Finally, I wish to record my sincere thanks to Paul McMahon, the managing editor at Paulist Press, for his invaluable guidance and support.

Stephen Prosser
Llandeilo, Wales
September 2008

Preface

Spencer Johnson's best-selling book *Who Moved My Cheese?*[1] is not really a book about cheese at all—it's a book about the inevitability of change and the different responses people make to those changes in their lives. Yes, of course, the whole book is based on the metaphor of cheese, and the powerful change messages are constructed around the story of the search for cheese but, as the book's subtitle reminds the reader, the book is first and foremost "an amazing way to deal with change in your work and in your life." Anyone in doubt about the central message of the book need only reread the final summary to be reminded of its seven cardinal principles for dealing with change.

When I undertook the research for this book and wrote the early drafts, I did not make any connection with Spencer Johnson's book, a book I had read some three years before. Paul McMahon, Paulist Press's managing editor, saw the link at once and encouraged me to rewrite this preface and make changes mainly to the opening and closing chapters and to the book's title.

Once I reread *Who Moved My Cheese?* I saw the connection at once. A comment from one of the book's four characters almost leapt from the page: "We keep doing the same things over and over again and wonder why things don't get better. If this wasn't so ridiculous, it would be even funnier." Johnson's book also spoke to me about seeing things from a new perspective while holding on to one's cherished values. For those reasons, principally, my book has been called *You Can Move the Cheese!*, as the four principles expounded in part 2— the purposeful leader, the principled leader, the resolute leader, and the exemplary leader—encourage individuals and their companies to move on, to change, and to behave differently based on fundamental and long-standing values. This book's subtitle, *The Role of an Effective Servant-Leader*, takes forward a theme I wrote about in a previous book for Paulist Press, *To Be a Servant-Leader*.

Before amending my original draft I had to convince myself that I wasn't merely trying to jump on the bandwagon of the success of Spencer Johnson's work. As far as I am concerned that would have been unacceptable. Then it struck me—I had been down the route of using cheese as a metaphor previously. In *To Be a Servant-Leader* I quoted a colleague's comment on an early draft of that book: "It's a bit like trying to eat a whole Stilton. Stilton has a strong and very intense taste." (Stilton is a strong-tasting and rich English cheese.) My colleague continued: "Although I really like it, I can only have a few slices at a time. Your document is tasty, but very intense." The published book had the indigestible removed, but I wrote that "a whole Stilton" remained a most suitable metaphor, as the book was intended to provide the reader with a number of tasty servant-leadership morsels to chew on, to think about and, hopefully, to digest. My use of the cheese metaphor previously seemed to support the decision to continue with references to cheese in this book.

This book has three parts:

Part 1: Identifying the Opportunities. The first chapter is introductory and describes my survey of approximately six hundred organisations. It identifies four types of companies in terms of how they value their employees, and concludes by comparing these four types with the characters in Spencer Johnson's book. Chapter 2 contains examples of these enlightened companies and shows how their belief in the value of their employees leads them to practise what I have called five key people propositions. The third chapter encourages readers to believe they can make a meaningful difference within their places of work, for the benefit of all.

Part 2: The Role of an Effective Servant-Leader. This section identifies complementary ways of providing effective leadership within the company. The four chapters discuss how to become "The Purposeful Leader," "The Principled Leader," "The Resolute Leader," and finally "The Exemplary Leader." This is the main section of the book and will encourage serious reflection concerning suitable responses to the various challenges.

Part 3: Conclusion. Entitled "You Can Move the Cheese!", the final chapter challenges the reader to take action and make a difference. My hope is that this book will inspire people to become the persons they really want to be deep down in their hearts and, as a result of the changes in them, that others will benefit from the actions taken. One of Spencer Johnson's summary points asks, "What Would You Do If You Weren't Afraid?", and this book encourages readers to take bold and substantial steps in the direction of acting beyond their fear.

> I have seen the sun break through
> to illuminate a small field
> for a while, and gone my way
> and forgotten it. But that was the pearl
> of great price, the one field that had
> treasure in it. I realise now
> that I must give all that I have
> to possess it. Life is not hurrying
> on to a receding future, nor hankering after
> an imagined past. It is the turning
> aside like Moses to the miracle
> of the lit bush, to a brightness
> that seemed as transitory as your youth,
> once, but is the eternity that awaits you.
> —*The Bright Field,* R. S. Thomas[a]

---

a. *Collected Poems: 1945–1990* (London: J. M. Dent, Orion Publishing Group, 2001).

PART 1

IDENTIFYING
THE
OPPORTUNITIES

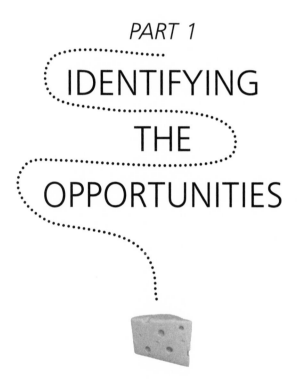

CHAPTER 1
Facing the Challenges

··

What Has Microsoft Discovered?

Anyone who regularly reads a variety of journals and newspapers and scans through numerous others cannot fail to be impressed by the sheer quantity and quality of Microsoft's advertising campaigns. As I started thinking about this book and wrote the first drafts, it seemed that their advertisements were in every journal and newspaper picked up, and the highly significant feature was the message they were communicating by means of their campaign.

Under the generic banner of "Microsoft™ the People-Ready Business™," a series of advertisements communicated to the reader that through the use of Microsoft's products it was possible to empower the people in the company to achieve far greater results. The advertisement headlines proclaimed that, "A people-ready business bets on its most important asset"©, and the narrative explained to the reader that:

> When you give your people tools that connect, inform, and empower them, they're ready. Ready to make the most of their knowledge, skill, and ambition.
>
> Your people are your company's most important asset.
>
> The key to building a people-ready business™ starts with investing in, relying on, and caring about your people's impact on your business.©

3

And the pièce de résistance came in one of the smaller advertisements in which Microsoft CEO Steve Ballmer was quoted as saying: "Empowering your people will empower the entire company"©.[a]

This represented wonderful news: an advertising campaign from a major company that placed the employees of a business at the very heart of its sales pitch. Wonderful news perhaps, but I confess the focus of the Microsoft message surprised me considerably: this was a company, known worldwide for its technology, who were emphasising that it is the people of an organisation who are its most important commodity, to use such a word to describe people. The Microsoft message emphasised that since people are so important, so critically important, to the success of a venture, then they should receive the best in information-management support. Whether or not Microsoft is the best product supplier is a marketing claim I am not able to judge, but that is not the main point of interest. What intrigued me is that Microsoft decided to emphasise people—not technology but people, not efficiency per se but people—and their marketing approach was fascinating for the simple reason that I could not agree more with such sentiments.

Admittedly, too much reliance should not be placed on the evidence of the advertising policy of just one company (although there are other similar examples), but it is fascinating when one of the world's commercial giants focuses their marketing effort on emphasising the importance of the people in a business. It makes the reader think about what Microsoft might know concerning trends within the workplace and the economy at large: have they discovered that companies are waking up to the fact that it really is their people who represent their true competitive advantage; that companies are realising, at long last for many of them, that much of their competitive advantage lies in the quality and contribution of their people; and is the Microsoft organisation targeting its marketing efforts towards this growing realisation?

---

a. I have done my very best to honour stringent copyright restrictions. This and subsequent Steve Ballmer views are from www.microsoft.com and were extracted on April 21, 2006.

With these thoughts in mind I asked three important initial questions:

Is there a growing number of companies who treat their people as truly valuable assets?

If there is, then what are the lessons for other companies?

How can leaders be in the vanguard of leadership for their people?

I was intrigued, and an examination of the Microsoft Web site found page after page that demonstrated their belief in the value of people within organisations. Understandably, the emphasis in the Web pages was principally a marketing message, but that does not devalue the clear overall message concerning the importance placed on the people within a company:

Organization doesn't really accomplish anything. Plans don't accomplish anything either. Theories of management don't much matter. Endeavors succeed or fail because of the people involved.—Colin Powell[b]

The best businesses work very hard to facilitate their people's success.—Steve Ballmer

The variety of material on the Microsoft Web site led to an examination of other businesses to see if a trend could be spotted—a trend that would show a growing number of organisations who were genuinely treating their people as if they were the most important assets within the company.

Survey

Over six hundred Web sites were examined, including those of companies listed on Wall Street, the Top 100 Shares, the Fastest Growing New Companies, the 100 Best Companies to Work For (in

---

b. Oren Harari, *The Leadership Secrets of Colin Powell* (New York: McGraw-Hill, 2002).

the UK), and many other businesses based on their traditions and corporate reputation. I made sure that the companies were representative of different sectors of the economy, including banking and finance, construction and engineering, health and pharmaceuticals, industrials, retailing, technology and telecommunications, and what is generically known as utilities. The companies chosen were also a mixture of large and small businesses, some operated solely in the US or the UK, and others internationally.

The information from the snapshot survey of businesses provided evidence of the range of different priorities and practices existing in these companies. Furthermore, the information highlighted the existence of companies across different sectors that do their best to treat their people with respect and in a way that maximises the growth and contribution of the individual and, in turn, the company's full potential.

Before the findings are presented four important caveats must be mentioned. First, this was not a comprehensive survey, as one would expect in a major research project; mine was a snapshot of practices across a wide spectrum of companies at a given point in time. Second, it is not suggested that the businesses used to illustrate the points of principle considered later are necessarily exemplary organisations in everything they do, or that they represent excellence in terms of bottom-line performance, or that they should form the basis of an investment portfolio or some such thing. They may be, but then again they may not be. Third, this survey relied on the evidence supplied on the company Web sites, and this runs the risk of my being charged with naiveté in taking what companies have to say at face value. I contend that this is not naiveté on my part, that I innocently believed everything a Web site told me, but rather it is a recognition that there are companies who at the very least feel the need to express themselves in a form that signals their belief in the critical importance of their people. I am prepared to take reasonable risks in using these companies in order to illustrate a principle or practice, and I would remind any cynic that these examples do not suggest that they are perfect organisations or that they are necessarily examples of the best businesses in the world. Fourth, inevitably there will be academics and commentators who will claim that these companies are only interested in people because it helps them to make more dollars or pounds. In reply I ask those sceptical academics and commentators to explore honestly, without political prejudice or class bias, the reasons for the principles and actions of these and other such companies. Without a doubt, profit is a motive—without profit they would cease to exist—but there is something fundamentally different about these companies, and that has chiefly to do with their relationship with their people.

Finally, and in relation to all four caveats, I want to emphasise that this was a search for evidence, no matter how small, that there are companies in most sectors of the economy who display a genuine belief that their employees really are their most important resource. That is sufficient evidence for what I have to say later in the book, where I suggest the means by which any type of company, or more significantly individual leaders within a company, can treat people in much the same way. Surely that is a goal worthy of further exploration.

Findings

The analysis revealed that the six hundred plus businesses could be conveniently classified into four main categories. It is unnecessary and unhelpful to identify the exact numbers of businesses placed in each category, as that would run the risk of suggesting a precision based on a quantitative assessment over a longer period, and it is sufficient to provide a short description of each of the four company categories:

Category 1—A number of Web sites were dominated by details of the company's product, irrespective of sector: some promoted engineering, some retail products, others technological innovations and so on. Not only was the home page of the Web site dominated by the product, which would be understandable for companies trying to sell their products, but the entire Web site was dedicated to what the business produced and what they sold. In these sites, when the "About Us" or "Careers" or "Vision and Values" pages were explored there was still a clear impression that this was a company that concentrated on its manufacturing, distributive, or research capacities, and the fact that they also employed people appeared to be almost coincidental. The impression given was that the employees of the business were merely another component in the manufacturing, service, or commodity processes, and therefore it was reasonable to conclude that for these companies their employees had no inherent worth and certainly were not seen as key to the growth of the business. These Web sites gave the impression that the companies' products were everything and that their employees were merely one of the many resources needed in order to deliver the final product. The employees were just another cost factor in the profit and loss account, just like any other raw material.

Category 2—The companies falling within this category comprised those with problem Web sites, which, despite representing commercially active companies, were dreadful and counterproductive. They were often inaccessible, or when finally arrived at, said little of worth or were difficult to use and became a frustrating experience. Further, some gave no recognition at all of the presence of people within their company—it was as if they had no employees. They were astonishingly poor sites, and it makes one wonder whether their CEO and senior management team ever took time to examine the image conveyed to potential customers. There is little doubt that some of the sites were having technical problems on the day they were examined, but there were far too many of these poor sites for it to be merely a temporary technological blip and, in any case, I made a point of returning to a number of them. In many instances the technological access worked perfectly well; it was just that the sites did a dreadful job in communicating worthwhile information about any aspect of the company, not to mention its people policies.

Category 3—These companies demonstrated commitment to an integrated and comprehensive system of human resource management (HRM). Some of the HRM systems were up-to-date and sophisticated, even leading edge in many instances, while others appeared to be fairly standard and reminiscent of those found in businesses in the mid-1980s. The more sophisticated systems had the very latest in HRM techniques, and the companies' HR departments should be commended for their practices. Yet the language used to describe their overall approach to the management of people often did not emphasise, or even suggest, that they really believed their employees were their most important asset, even when their Web sites declared that their people were indeed just that. Words alone were not sufficient evidence to convince me; there was a need to see some "proof" that the rhetoric had been converted into tangible practice. These companies were sophisticated practitioners of human resource management; they wanted to get the most out of their people for business reasons—no bad thing, in and of itself, and there was much to commend the organisations. There was, however, little sense of a deep-rooted appreciation that it was their people who ultimately made the company a success or a failure.

Category 4—On these company Web sites it was possible to read what they had to say about their people and to feel proud. It was crystal clear that they were companies who really believed that their people were of the utmost importance and that without them the business would be a poorer place. There was something beyond even that conviction: these companies appeared to believe in people, they believed they had a mission to do the very best for their people, and they believed that by focusing on the contribution of their people they could build the business further. That is an important and fundamental distinction—these were not businesses that planned to invest substantially in their people if and when they had sufficient resources, but these were companies who believed that by investing substantially in their employees, wherever possible, the people and the business would prosper as a direct result of that investment.

To be a company that believes in people, to attempt to do the best for one's employees, and to possess a firm conviction that focusing on the contribution of one's staff will build the business is some statement of faith, and that is exactly the general approach taken by these companies. Seldom do the individual companies make grandiose-sounding claims, but what is evident is that they believe their people are important in and of themselves and are an essential component of the organisation's success.

Examples of these category 4 companies are shown in the next chapter, and I am only too well aware (as I hinted earlier) that to list those companies runs the risk of being a fool who rushes in where angels fear to tread! The dangers are well known: no sooner are examples cited than those very companies may be engaged in staffing problems, or their stock market performance may become parlous, or some of their directors may be sacked or indicted. The problems are notorious to any researcher and writer who believes examples need to be provided. For these and other reasons, there was a temptation to remove the names of the companies, and I have yielded to this temptation where there was little point in naming them; but where attempting to hide their identity became pointless, as the briefest description of their activities would allow the reader to identify the company, I have used the business's name. So, I suppose I have taken a measured (or perhaps inevitable) risk.

In the next chapter I turn to these examples, but before doing so I need to say something about the main challenges a leader may face if he or she wishes to bring about changes in the way people are valued and treated.

Facing the Personal Challenge of Change

In some ways, the four company categories I identified reflect the four characters in Spencer Johnson's *Who Moved My Cheese?* as reflected by their different reactions to change: category 4 companies have readily embraced the need to recognise the intrinsic value of their people, while category 3 companies appear to be heading in that direction by means of their HR policies and practice; many category 1 companies need much persuasion to change their understanding of the true worth of people and, quite frankly, category 2 companies are beyond the pale and unlikely to change. It almost goes without saying that the fit between Johnson's four characters and their attitudes towards change and my four company categories and the attitude towards people that they display is not nearly exact. If it were, some form of manipulation on my part might well have been suspected;

also, Johnson's book contains numerous other important dimensions and principles concerning change.

As I read his book for the second and third time and thought about what I had discovered in my category 4 companies, it encouraged me to think long and hard about the challenges a leader faces in bringing about a transformation in the way people are valued and treated within the company. Johnson, on the first page of the book, describes the challenges facing all types of individuals committed to change:

> Whatever parts of us we choose to use, we all share something in common: a need to find our way in the maze and succeed in changing times.

So how do leaders find their way through the maze of organisational life? How can they experience success, or at the very least minimise the chances of failure, as they strive to bring about change for the benefit of people and the company? There is no foolproof, ready-made solution, but as I continued to think about the four leadership dimensions set out in the second part of this book, Johnson's work encouraged further thought about some general introductory principles that provide meaningful guidance for the leader facing the challenges of change. The following five points are my words and thoughts, and are often written in the style of maxims, but many of the ideas were generated as a result of Johnson's stimulating insights.

1. ACCEPT THE INEVITABILITY OF CHANGE

Change is a common experience. As the new-old cliché expresses it: change is the only constant in life. For some, change is exciting—they love the thrill of it; for others it is a source of apprehension and they can do without it. Most people, however, just learn that change is inevitable and that adopting a flexible attitude towards change is far better than an inflexible, intransigent attitude. In other words, it is better to be like a surfer riding the waves of change than to be like King Canute, who did his best to hold back the arrival of the inevitable sea waves.

At times change can be stressful, although change that removes existing unacceptable conditions is usually most welcome. If someone expects change to happen, then they are less likely to be surprised by it and more likely to cope with it, but if they do not anticipate change then they may become like the proverbial boiled frog: it is said that if a frog is placed in a pan of hot water it will jump out, but if it is placed in a pan of cold water and the temperature is increased gradually, then in time the frog will be boiled.

Anyone exercising a leadership role within a company should be prepared for change. The relationship of the leader to the follower is changing rapidly, and it really is sensible to accept and even welcome the arrival of change and alter one's leadership style wherever necessary.

2. BE SPECIFIC ABOUT CHANGE OBJECTIVES

Try not to be one of those people who amble through life without any idea about what it is they are trying to achieve—the more they stroll around the more aimless their life becomes. Wherever possible, it is important to have a picture of what needs to be achieved, and some people do this by describing what they want their future to be like. To help them with this task they make use of their five senses: what will it look like, feel like, sound like, taste like, and even smell like—which seems quite apposite given the fact that one of Johnson's main characters is called Sniff.

The same exercise can be applied to the companies. It can help to define the type of organisation to strive for and the sort of employers they wish to be. Leaders within such companies will have plans that recognise the contribution of their people in genuine ways, without reverting to the oft quoted and often meaningless maxim that "our people are our greatest resource."

3. UNDERSTAND WHAT MOTIVATES PEOPLE

To be an effective leader capable of motivating other people, there must first be an understanding of what motivates him or her. Leaders must know their own personalities and how they react to change; the difference between how they react to change and how they should react; what they really want to get out of life; what things they value and do not value; and their attitude to the work they perform. There is much else to be learned, but this represents a sound start.

The next thing to consider is how well they know the people they lead and the differences that make them individuals rather than some amorphous mass known as employees. How do they want to be led? What is their attitude towards work—is it the be-all and end-all of life for them? How can they be helped to feel valued? What makes them feel good about the jobs they do? And much more.

If a leader really wants to provide a work environment where people believe they are key assets and encouraged to give of their best, that allows them to express themselves and develop as people, where they can feel that they have sufficient personal development and authority, then it is essential that their needs be met. I am not suggesting that the company should suddenly become a philanthropic society established solely for the benefit of its employees, but it does mean that leaders are investing properly in the individual needs of their people because they understand that it is one of the best investments they can make.

4. BE HONEST ABOUT NEGATIVE REACTIONS

For many leaders, the most likely reaction to the prospect of change is fear: fear of the unknown, what the change will mean, whether they will be able to cope or not and, in this context, fear of what it will mean to them if they genuinely show people that they are their organisations' most important assets. Fear of the unknown is quite understandable, and a certain amount of apprehension is much to be preferred to the attitudes of the change junkies who must have their latest adrenalin rush by constructing a series of changes. It is far better to take a measured approach to change, one that is planned over a period of time. Sudden change should be reserved for emergency circumstances wherever possible.

Another frequent response to the need for change is what I call the fallacy of activity. Activity is not necessarily the same as progress, and yet many people respond to the need for change by engaging in strenuous work that does not take them forward. I love the story [2] of a colonel who, in an end-of-tour report, described his having to deal with a lack of proper planning and strategy as "pasting feathers together, hoping for a duck." He had been extremely busy, but there was little sense of a meaningful strategy. To make real progress in bringing about change there is always need for an effective plan, and no amount of activity and sheer hard work will fool anyone when expected progress is not being made.

5. STICK TO VALUES

During periods of change, when decisions have to be made often without possession of all of the facts or against a tight timescale, it is essential to be sure of one's principles and the underlying values that guide. Much of what follows in part 2 of this book is based on such values, and during periods of change they provide a solid anchor in one's life; they furnish a framework against which actions can be assessed; they help an individual move forward with greater confidence; and they provide an agenda for open debate on the actions to be taken. This is not some simple formulaic answer, but I am asking the reader to consider an appropriate and sensitive application of fundamental values in the belief that they will help transform the leadership of the organisation and thereby help meet the needs of many.

CHAPTER 2

Exploring a Company's Strengths

....

Category 4 companies have much to commend them, and they provide encouragement to those interested in creating organisations that value people. A closer examination of the companies led to the discovery of five key people propositions that characterise the organisations in one way or another. Some of the companies possess a number of these common characteristics; some have all of them, but no matter the number of key people propositions, each of the organisations is representative of a distinctive type of enterprise: a company that believes in its people.

The five key people propositions are described briefly and then exemplified by reference to a sample of category 4 companies. Certain companies could have been used to illustrate more than one of the people propositions, but only one reference is made to each organisation for reasons of brevity and clarity and, as explained in chapter 1, sometimes the company is named and sometimes it is not.

People Proposition 1:
A Genuine Belief in Their People

As might be expected, the first prominent characteristic of category 4 companies is a genuine belief in the merits of their people—their staff. There appears to be an authentic belief that the people employed in the company are their greatest asset, although these businesses will often refrain from uttering the cliché and mantra, "Our people are our greatest asset." They have no need to say such a thing, as it is evident in the way the company is organised and in how work is conducted. They are companies who believe that if the business wants to survive and thrive, then this "resource," probably above all others, needs to be nurtured. It is their people who provide the intellectual drive, who make things happen, who provide customer satisfaction, and who generate the essential profits needed for further investment. As such they invest in the ongoing development of their people, encourage them to reach their full potential, and see them as genuine stakeholders within the business. On occasion, this stakeholder concept becomes tangible through the establishment of some form of employee ownership.

❖

The Air Products company was founded in 1940 in Michigan to produce and sell industrial gases on one site. Today, the company is in more than thirty countries, with 18,500 employees around the world, and customers in technology, energy, healthcare, and industrial markets using its products, a range of gas and associated goods. The organisation prides itself for its company culture, the standards of its operations, and its commitment to the environment. Product research backs up their claim that their competitive advantage is based on the quality and characteristics of their people. The company even goes as far as to claim that the qualities and behaviour of their people create the personality and thereby the success of the company. As such, they encourage their people to achieve their full potential.

❖

In fairness to law firms, I was spoilt for choice in selecting which legal business to include in this illustrative list, as so many of them emphasise commitment to their employees and maintain that it is their people alone who provide the principal competitive advantage. One such company, a large and successful law firm with offices in many English cities, is proud to claim that the key to their success is their people. They emphasise the importance of their employees and place great value on them as demonstrated by recognition of their expertise, professionalism, passion, and dedication. The company Web site says of its employees: "…going the all-important extra mile is second nature"—an interesting phrase, given the points I wish to make in the second part of this book. As a company they also emphasise the importance of their values base.

❖

This UK-based construction company was formed in 1956 with only four on the staff and today employs over five hundred people. The business strap line proclaims that "The difference is our people," and it is one of the few companies in the UK to be wholly owned by its employees. The company believes that this ownership provides for better customer service and quality of product. Their philosophy is disarmingly simple and no doubt effective: if the staff are happy and skilled at what they do, then they look after the customers who, in turn, are happy and return with more business, which makes the staff (who are the shareholders) happy—simple, yet effective. The sense of the company being based on the concept of togetherness is reinforced by "regular group days for relaxation and involving the family in your work" and a variety of sporting and social events.

❖

3M is a company hardly needing introduction. It supplies technological products to a variety of sectors of the economy and with worldwide sales in excess of $20 billion, seventy thousand employees, and a presence in over sixty countries, this is truly a global enterprise. Its values include the rather touching and commendable aspiration to be "a company employees are proud to be part of." Of particular significance is their commitment to the notion of 3M leadership based on a belief that "investing in our people is most important" and that "if your people grow, your company will grow." They believe it is possible to make a connection between the growth and development of the individuals within the company and the provision of products and services that the customers value, thereby contributing to the growth and development of the business. As such, effective leadership remains a key priority for the company, and the development of ideas based on the talent and imagination of their employees is also high on their agenda. Within their culture of innovation there is the active reception of ideas from its entire people, and there is provision for staff to pursue ideas even if they fall outside a person's normal job. (The story behind the invention of Post-it® Notes within 3M has become a part of general organisational folklore.) 3M is actively involved in community events and supports a variety of initiatives through its people—current and retired employees—and has won a number of prestigious awards for its work in this field.

❖

William Hesketh Lever wanted to promote cleanliness and hygiene in the England of Queen Victoria's time and, in the late nineteenth century, formed the company that one day would become Unilever. Today, Unilever sets out to achieve its mission to "...add vitality to life" through a range of brands that meet needs in the nutrition, hygiene, and personal care market sectors. One of their beliefs is that: "We grow as a company by growing our people," and it is this belief that motivates the company to keep their people "...fulfilled and committed." This commitment drives their regular worldwide employee surveys which, in turn, feed into their business-planning processes. This means that the Unilever people are at the centre of all business activities, including their "professional fulfilment" and "work/life balance." They consider the company to be a community rather than a corporate body, and a community "...shaped and led by its people." As one would expect, especially within a community, there is a corporate standard of exhibiting the best behaviour towards the people they work with and towards the communities and environment they influence.

People Proposition 2: A Work Environment That Promotes Family and Fun and Celebrates Success

These companies try to create a work environment that is fun to be in and one that resembles a family—in fact, the words *fun* and *family* are often two of the prominent words on their Web sites. To achieve these aims a number of events are planned to encourage fun, and physical and relational working conditions are structured to promote a sense of family. There is a strong belief that having happy staff who enjoy their work makes for satisfied customers and, in turn, a business that is financially profitable and emotionally healthy.

The concept of fun and family is not divorced from the realities of running a company, and interpersonal goals are complemented by a strong commitment to performance, especially when related to meeting the needs of the customer—customer service is a business imperative. As part of their commitment to customers there is dedication to quality, and employees are encouraged to become engaged in innovation. As one might imagine, external and internal awards and accolades are celebrated rigorously and enthusiastically, as such events fulfil the desire to have fun, be family, and provide first-rate customer service through quality service and products.

❖

One of Britain's leading direct-response car insurance companies, selling insurance directly to the customer, commenced trading in January 1993 with one product, no customers, and less than sixty employees. Less than four years later the business owned six products and had in excess of one million customers and two thousand employees. The company culture is relaxed and friendly, and although there is a commitment to individual growth through training and development, the culture seems to be epitomised by its "Ministry of Fun": an enterprise established to arrange events, both internally and externally, designed to make the company a fun place to work. The company believes that if its employees are happy and enjoying their work, then their happiness and enjoyment will be transferred to their transactions with customers. They believe in a simple yet successful circle of happy employees leading to happy customers, leading to happy investors, leading to a happy business. And it appears to be working extremely well in practice. One of the company's core values is its belief that everyone connected with the business, whether they are suppliers or the community or customers or employees, is a stakeholder in the business. Unexpectedly, the company values its customers above all else, and this drives the "can-do" attitude within the business. Within the local community it sponsors a number of events to demonstrate to all stakeholders the nature of the company, including its spirit of fun and community involvement. Moreover, the company's CEO created the eponymous Henry's Pot. The Pot gives financial support to a range of charities and other organisations associated with the staff and their families. Within its Quality Measures Programme there are annual awards given to the most successful departments, and the Programme drives a part of the annual Staff Profit Share.

❖

A well-known car rental company operating in many countries of the world believes that their claim to be a family may "sound corny," but their statements of values and cultures demonstrate their fundamental belief. Interestingly, their career opportunities advertisement specifies quite openly and commendably that potential employees will need to be sure that they "fit" within those values and culture. Their values statement includes such principles as passion, courage, modesty (based on the concept of teamwork and collective praise), and loyalty, and their culture statements underpin these values, with phrases emphasising teamwork, working with velocity, competing to win, and keeping promises. These sentiments encourage the employees to see themselves as a family; to collaborate and cooperate rather than compete; to emphasise trust and sincerity in their dealings with one another; and to recognise their commitment to the environment and the larger communities around them. In terms of the various local communities, they set out to be role models for other companies, and they encourage employee involvement in civic and charitable work.

❖

Marriott is another company that hardly needs to be introduced, since its hotels and hospitality services in approximately seventy countries across the world are well known. Its values are built around the concept of the Marriott Way, and its fundamental belief is that its ongoing business success will be achieved by serving its employees, who are known as associates, its customers, and the wider community. Associates (staff) are provided with a range of development opportunities based on the company's "unshakeable conviction that our people are our most important asset." Personal growth and development, a commitment to staff who are "ethical and trustworthy," and a "homelike atmosphere and friendly workplace relationships" are key to the company and its success. At the very heart of the organisation is the unshakeable belief that it is their people who represent success or failure for the business. They even go so far as stating that their people are "…the foundation of Marriott's success for over 75 years!" The company is also actively involved in a number of community and sustainable environment projects through its "Spirit to Serve Our Communities" and "Green Marriott" programmes.

❖

One of America's best-known fashion retailers, founded in the early twentieth century, has remained committed to the principle of "earning the trust of our customers, one at a time." The company has a guiding set of values that conform to its reputation for customer service, quality of product, and overall value. Although a publicly quoted company, a strong family presence remains in the running of the business that inculcates a family atmosphere into the management style, encouraging staff to "…celebrate our achievements and appreciate one another—just like family." Employees have a financial and personal interest in the company and are encouraged to behave positively to one another and to the community around them. Honesty and respect are valued, as is kindness to one another and to customers—"Treat others as you'd like to be treated" is one of their tenets for doing business—they recognise meritorious performance and support numerous community events. Notably, employees are encouraged to have fun, and there is an open-door policy for the discussion of various issues, since the company wants to ensure that employees feel "…valued, welcomed, and cared for."

❖

A global company, founded between the two world wars, specialises in products for the food, beverage, household, and body-care markets. A number of its products bear popular names. It is this company's belief that their people and culture, two inextricably linked factors, make their organisation special. This talented workforce is characterized by a strong sense of family, with employees apparently (and this sounds like a typical "motherhood and apple pie" expression) referring to the company with the remark, "It's my business." In terms of the people they set out to recruit and the work environment they create, a commitment to quality is paramount, and the company ethos is one where people care about how they treat one another, including an emphasis on the "…highest standards of ethical conduct in every aspect of their work." They also want a workplace where people can grow in terms of their career and personal life, while maintaining a balance between their work, their families, and the communities in which they live.

People Proposition 3: An Emphasis on Fundamental Principles and Values

Characteristic 3 is a clear statement of the values or principles of a particular company and the way in which these values or principles drive each part of business activity. In turn, the values have an impact on the culture of the organisation, and this culture is reflected in the policies and practices that are developed.

In most cases, the language used on their Web sites and in their documentation is different despite the fact that many of the companies are bastions of a traditional view of the world. There is frequent use of terms such as *sustainable, spiritual, moral, passion, respect, dignity* and *ethical,* and the way in which the words are used leads the reader to believe they are meant. These words and the concepts they represent often find their way into the brochures of other established businesses as they enter another century of activity. For some, it is as if they are finding courage through the actions of others to speak about principles they have practised for many generations.

❖

Everyone knows Colgate. It started when William Colgate launched a small soap and candle business in New York City and developed it into a successful business with a global presence. It is a company that believes its success is linked to the strength and innovation of its people, especially in their ability to transform the business and exploit new opportunities. Colgate's business activities are governed by three principal values—caring, global teamwork, and continuous improvement—and the caring value is associated with its employees (the significance of placing employees first should be highlighted), customers, shareholders, and business partners. In its activities the business is committed to acting with "compassion, integrity and honesty in all situations, to listen with respect to others and to value differences." Through their "Valuing Colgate People" training programme the shared values are reinforced and, encouragingly, one of the main objectives is to "recognize, value and respect the unique contributions each person brings to Colgate." Their belief in their people being their greatest resource, so often a hollow phrase in some other organisations, is reinforced by their personnel practices, such as their Becoming the Best Place to Work initiatives and their Managing with Respect initiative, which aims to create and encourage "an environment of trust and community." Within this initiative's five principles is the intriguing "Valuing Unique Contributions." A message from the company's senior officials (chairman and chief executive officer, president and chief operating officer, vice chairman, and vice president of global business practices and corporate social responsibility) is designed to emphasise the values-based approach and remind everyone that its values are "…the driving force behind everything we do."

❖

One century-old manufacturing and supplies company, respected for its innovations, design, specifications, and customer service, is a family-owned company. Their Web site demonstrates its commitment to the principle of listening to the customer and innovating to find acceptable solutions. They have developed a set of ten guiding principles to direct their corporate and individual actions. Although many of these principles can be found in numerous other organisations, their belief that work should be both enjoyable and rewarding and their wish to encourage employees to challenge the way things are done are worth noting. The ten principles are translated into a People Mission Statement and contain notable additions to the statements one would expect to find. These include the encouragement of people to achieve their potential, their involvement in decision-making, and the provision of a framework of learning and development.

❖

Another global company, founded in the early twentieth century, manufactures electrical systems and components for a range of uses across many sectors. Its electrical, fluid power, truck and automotive results are important factors in trading success, but their emphasis is on the way they conduct business, and they believe that it is their values and culture that define the organisation and govern the way they undertake their activities. Although it recognises that it exists to operate profitably for the benefit of its shareholders, it also believes that its ability to achieve those financial targets is best realised by a commitment to its core values. These concepts are fairly typical of companies committed to a set of meaningful values, and include "Treat each other with respect" and "Be fair, honest and open." These values translate into operational principles and the belief that superior performance can be best achieved when all employees, managers, and staff "share certain key beliefs about our mutual responsibilities to one another." Additionally, this culture encourages employees to realise their full potential and to expect their contributions to be praised and rewarded. Their company philosophy was constructed with the involvement of all of its employees from across the country and lays down a number of challenging operating principles, including an attempt to involve all employees in the development and continuing success of the business; the encouragement of lifelong learning; and the creation of an environment where the ideas of all are given the opportunity to flourish.

❖

With over two hundred operating companies, in excess of 100,000 staff, and a presence in numerous countries of the world, Johnson & Johnson is a major manufacturer of health-care products and provider of associated services. As a global business it has come a long way from the days when General Robert Wood Johnson set up a small family-owned business. Yet the business holds true to the views of its founder. In 1935, the prescient Johnson authored a document entitled *Try Reality*, in which he encouraged other industrial magnates to follow what he called, "a new industrial philosophy" calling for a genuine commitment to the company's staff, customers, the wider community, and, of course, its shareholders. A man of vision— a man ahead of his time. Johnson & Johnson is well known for its credo, written by Johnson in 1943—the alternative to a vision or mission statement that guides the actions of the company in all it does. This one-page document sets out its commitment: to clinicians, parents, and other consumers of its products; to fair trading principles; to all aspects of the employment relationship; to the development and proper management of the individual; to the community; and to stockholders. (This is the briefest description of their Credo, and it is worth reading the document in full to understand the comprehensive nature and the effect of such a statement within the company.) The Credo is translated into a set of values for the management of the business, ensuring, for example, the alignment of "success with things that are good for people" and that the decision-making process be ethical, which includes recognising "the moral issue" as one of its dimensions. This approach also ensures that the company's leaders are values-based people and, importantly, it is this commitment to a common set of values that allows the opportunity for a degree of autonomy amongst the employees of the company in their critical decision making. On a regular basis the effectiveness and applicability of the Credo in practice is evaluated.

❖

Ask most people about Wrigley's and two things come to mind: chewing gum and their architecturally iconic world headquarters building in Chicago, Illinois—the Wrigley Building. The company was founded in 1891 and has developed a range of well-known products. As a company, they believe that their associates (i.e., employees) "...are the most important part of our continued growth and success...." "The Wrigley Way" guides the behaviour of the associates. This set of principles and values acts as a compass to guide the practice of business and includes specific references to the position and role of its people. The values include references to the "... trust, dignity, and respect..." they show to one another, the commitment to the recruitment of first-class talented people and their lifelong learning, and the need to conduct business against a set of ethical standards.

People Proposition 4: An Enlightened Set of Human Resource Policies

The personnel or human resource (HR) systems of most category 4 companies are, in the main, fairly straightforward and typical of a company in their sector. Then one notices that the HR policies are often especially sensitive to allow for the promotion of the openness that exists in the employer-employee relationship. They are designed to meet the needs of the person and the business, and this construct is also intended to obviate and, if necessary, resolve the potential and possibly inevitable conflict that can arise in any human organisation. The HR policies are likely to contain sound and imaginative personal development opportunities, rapid promotion opportunities in return for outstanding performance, and a commitment to organisational learning that reinforces the commitment to growth of the enterprise and its commitment to its customers.

Many of the companies support the development of the individual and, as such, HR policies highlight the growth and reward of individuals rather than the whole of the workforce, although these benefits are available to all based on effort. As these companies wish to promote a sense of family, every effort is made to ensure that there is a felt fairness over the application of their HR policies and practices.

❖

An independent partnership of commercial property consultants was founded in 1725 by two brothers and is now based in a number of UK and other European capital cities. In over 275 years of business practice, embracing the concepts of continuity and change has been fundamental to their success, and they proudly state that: "the future success of our firm depends on the knowledge, ability, professionalism and motivation of all our staff." This belief is translated into actions to ensure that individuals reach their full potential. A range of personnel policies concerning recruitment, development, and reward, and many more are complemented by the commitment to innovation and creativity—"not being afraid to try something new." The firm has established an innovation unit to promote ideas, created a system of sabbaticals for certain staff, transformed its working environment through the DJ Café—where staff can "hold informal meetings, surf the net, read the papers, eat their lunch or just take five," and its efforts have brought it many accolades. As might be expected, it has a range of environment-friendly and corporate social responsibility policies and, most impressively, it is involved in a wide range of charitable and community support efforts.

❖

A travel business founded in Australia has become one of the world's largest independent travel retailers, with stores in the USA, UK, and many other countries. Highly significant is their belief that "our company is our people," and this belief is lived out through care for the "health and well being...personal and professional development...[and] financial security" of its people. They believe that they have not lost sight of the main ingredients of their success, such as: building a strong family like working ethos. They even refer to units within the organisation as a village or tribe! This commitment is reinforced through their egalitarian philosophy and what they call their "spiritual and physical commitment to empower ourselves personally and professionally." They claim this makes them unique, and certainly their belief in equal privileges for each individual sets them apart from most companies. They also lay great store on work being challenging and fun for all employees. Individuals have an opportunity to own a part of the company through the Business Ownership Scheme, and they contend that employees should see a "clear pathway to achieving their hopes, aspirations and dreams." Hard work is rewarded, but they also appear to value playing hard, and their social celebrations include "buzz nights, award ceremonies and team get togethers," and one of their guiding principles is "if your work isn't fun you shouldn't be doing it." To support their open performance culture they hold regular celebrations of achievement nationally and internationally.

❖

The John Lewis Partnership comprises twenty-six department stores, two hundred supermarkets, and a direct-services company. Most significantly, its 64,000 permanent staff are considered partners in the business, and the Partnership is the UK's largest and longest-lasting company based on the principle of worker coownership. All "Partners" take a share of the business's profits. The founder, John Spedan Lewis, was prepared to sacrifice his ownership of the company in order that current and future staff would be able to "experiment in industrial democracy" and allow his business to flourish without the pressure of external shareholders. His words contain a resounding challenge:

> The Partnership was meant to enable people to feel that they might be making a contribution of real value to the ceaseless experimenting that is necessary to human progress. It was meant for people who need not only something to live by but something to live for.

Wisely, Lewis set down his values as guiding principles for subsequent generations to follow. Many of the operating principles are what one would expect and include statements concerning the locus of power, the distribution of profits, the mutual respect among members, and a commitment to honesty and integrity in its transactions; but there are also some statements that almost take one's breath away:

> The Partnership's ultimate purpose is the happiness of all its members, through their worthwhile and satisfying employment in a successful business.

This concept translates into actions such as the support given to its members when they face such life trials as ill health, unexpected financial hardship, and retirement. There are also opportunities for sport and leisure, lifelong learning, and much else. John Spedan Lewis believed that his approach would attract top-class people into its management hierarchy and that the principles of the business, especially the commitment to the customer, would deliver benefits for the partners. The story of the Partnership suggests that this visionary was right.

❖

An international brewing company with many well-known brands operating in over sixty countries across the world sees its people as being the most important ingredient in their competitive position. They acknowledge the extent of competition in the brewing business and that all brewers use "…the same equipment, the same technology and the same suppliers," and so it is axiomatic to them that what truly differentiates a company is the talents and contribution of its people. Many of their HR policies and practices are standard for a global company, but the commitment to a talent strategy and what they call their Human Resource Proposition is worth noting. The Proposition assumes that the people within the company want to "…accept accountability and influence outcomes that shape the organisation…," and that they want to practice self-management; on this premise and others, a range of initiatives has been put in place. These initiatives include learning and development programmes and measures to help facilitate communication, collaboration, and the transfer of skills across the company and, indeed, across continents. Their practices are by no means unique, but what is worthy is their clear commitment to the notion that it is their people who make the greatest difference to their business—the business of brewing.

❖

A banking, insurance, and financial services business with over 23 million customers and 167,000 employees ("total team members") is one of the world's largest private employers. Their business statements contain numerous significant beliefs in the value of their people. To achieve their overall business vision they have identified ten strategic initiatives, and one of these sees their "people as a competitive advantage." Because of this belief they invest in their human capital and believe it to be "...the most important, valuable investment we can make." Understandably, they attempt to recruit quality staff, develop them, encourage them to perform, and expect them to have fun. Their approach is distinctive and appealing:

> When our people are in the right jobs, spending time on the right things, managed well, feeling good about their contributions, fully using their skills and learning new ones, and having fun—they'll do it right for the customer.

They also expend effort in demonstrating to staff that the company believes in them as people. Within its extensive description of values and their importance is an emphasis on hearing the views of staff through regular surveys, an encouragement of leadership at all levels (and especially in terms of customer service), the identification and dissemination of best practices, and developing and recognising the contribution of employees.

People Proposition 5:
A Commitment to Corporate Social
Responsibility and Charitable Work

Many of these companies have meaningful corporate social responsibility programmes demonstrating a genuine commitment to the environment. For some it may represent initial and perhaps faltering steps in that direction; for others the commitment to act responsibly is entrenched in the way they do business. As discussions continue among world leaders concerning major environmental issues, it is right to ponder whether sufficient action is being taken to protect the world's resources, but that recognition should not undervalue the long-standing efforts of many of these companies to make a genuine and significant difference to the protection of the planet.

Additionally, many of these companies involve themselves in local and national charitable work, either corporately or through the efforts of individuals who are then sponsored by their colleagues and the company.

❖

One High Street jeweller, apart from its understandable belief in the quality of its merchandise, describes itself as having a "passion for people." Encouragingly and warmly, they state their belief in "treating people the way we'd like to be treated ourselves," a concept that has been around for at least two millennia but one that is refreshing when found on a corporate Web site. Their philosophy and values statements are what one would expect to find in such a company, but it is their list of commitments that makes the most interesting reading. Amongst the expected development and communication commitments are phrases such as, "Tell the total truth faster," "Encourage each other through recognition and praise," and "Celebrate our success." What is most remarkable about the company within this key people proposition is their commitment to charitable giving: the company donates 10 percent of their post-tax profits to charitable bodies. The company's staff are actively involved in local charity events, and the business sponsors a 10K Fun Run in addition to other events. They also pay attention to taking care of their own people.

❖

A leading property company, with a multibillion-pound investment portfolio, eighteen hundred employees, a large development programme, and a sixty-year track record is certainly well on its way to achieving its vision. The company considers its employees as key to its success and, as such, sets out to attract first-class people to its business, to appreciate their contribution and help them to grow as people within the organisation. The company is committed to a set of values as a central plank of its culture and has instituted a "Values into Action" programme. The values are in accordance with a customer and employee focused company, and the way in which these values are reinforced within the business is significant. To emphasise the importance of the values, quarterly and annual awards are made "to celebrate people who…demonstrate these values." The company's people strategy values continuous learning and development, and they attempt to demonstrate that they are a learning organisation and that the learning that takes place is fed into the business-strategy process. Interestingly, there is also a company "academy" to help facilitate this learning process. The company has set up a foundation to enable it to engage with the wider community in various activities. These activities can involve employee volunteering and charitable support, including support of a local school.

❖

Another company, a large firm of private mortgage insurers undertaking business principally in the US, Australia, New Zealand, and Europe, has been in existence for over thirty years. It's a fast-growing company, and in addition to maintaining a high quality of customer service, it believes that "…people are critical to a company's success." On the basis of this belief, they have created a working environment that is conducive to everyone giving of their best, and the company claims it "…goes the extra mile…" to motivate or, as they say, energise the workforce, and they have developed their own "university" to meet the learning needs of their staff. External development programmes are also financed. They emphasise the mission of the company and see their role in developing and extending the ownership of homes, both in the US and overseas, as laudable. The company mission is promoted further through a variety of community activities, working with nonprofit organisations and neighbourhood associations, and through their work with disadvantaged groups. For employees there is a family feel to the organisation—they call themselves the Family—and they promote what they call the Vibe: where work is to be seen as fun, with hard work complemented by a good atmosphere that makes the workplace welcoming. They go even further than this and believe that the company will go out of its way, well beyond the attractive employment package, to "...look out for..." its staff.

❖

This company traces its history back to a founder who took what was then a small opportunity and developed it into what became a major business operation. Over sixty years ago the founder drove his truckload of foodstuffs to Chicago, where he believed he would receive a better price for his consignment. He was right, and from those humble roots the business began to grow. Today the company is the largest provider of meat products in the world (according to its publicity material). The company is committed to meaningful employee development, to a partnership committed to ending hunger in America, and to environmental principles targeted at the communities in which their people live and work. What really sets them apart is their list of values, which includes: striving to be "honourable people," a company that "...operates with integrity and trust in all we do"; "a faith-friendly company"; and one that endeavours to "...honour God and be respectful of each other...."

Conclusion

These five key people propositions epitomise the category 4 companies:

1. A genuine belief in their people
2. A work environment that promotes family and fun and cele-brates success
3. An emphasis on fundamental principles and values
4. An enlightened set of human resource policies
5. A commitment to corporate social responsibility and chari-table work

The examples of the propositions in action come from a variety of companies, and there is no suggestion that these companies are exemplary in every action they undertake. However, they do illus-trate the existence of numerous companies with an impressive com-mitment to the importance of their people and their role within the wider community.

CHAPTER 3
Making the Right Decisions

· ·

> The trouble with the world is that the stupid are cocksure
> and the intelligent are full of doubt.
> —Bertrand Russell[a]

Are you willing to help *move the cheese*? Let me explain what I mean
before you respond.

Earlier, I explained how a comment from one of the four characters in Spencer Johnson's *Who Moved My Cheese?* almost leapt from
the page:

> We keep doing the same things over and over again and
> wonder why things don't get better. If this wasn't so ridicu-
> lous, it would be even funnier.

I went on to explain that Johnson's characters emphasise the
need to see things from a new perspective, and that encouraged me
to call this book *You Can Move the Cheese!*, since the four servant-
leadership dimensions expounded in part 2—the purposeful leader,
the principled leader, the resolute leader, and the exemplary leader—
encourage individuals and their companies to move on, to change,
and to behave differently in line with fundamental and long-standing
values.

When I ask, "Are you willing to help *move the cheese*?," the word
cheese represents the changes taking place in those companies that
recognise the intrinsic worth of their people and ensure every opportunity for their growth and much more. To *move the cheese* means to

---

a. Taken from brainyquote.com, March 3, 2009.

position the company, or the part of the company where you exercise influence, in line with this informed view of people and their worth.

Therefore, this final chapter of part 1 contains a fundamental challenge: it encourages you to think seriously about whether you are willing to make a real difference in the place where you work; it invites you to consider whether you are prepared to become a person who helps to *move the cheese* in a way that brings benefit to your colleagues and to you; it asks you to think about the contribution you can make, about the influence you can have on people. There are no grandiose claims concerning the results of such actions, but I do believe that if enough people took similar actions, then those (small or large) deeds would have a profound effect in bringing vibrancy to companies that currently appear sad and soulless places to work, and allow individuals to grow into the types of people they can become: energised, purposeful, and satisfied.

To *move the cheese* is an invitation to become enlightened and to join the ranks of those who relate to their colleagues as if they really are the most important assets within a company. Gandhi may have used hyperbole when he said, "The difference between what we are doing and what we're capable of doing would solve most of the world's problems," but imagine what would happen in your company if you and everyone else tapped into the potential residing in your friends and colleagues. Can you imagine the change that might take place?

Some people may think I have my head in the clouds; that I am a woolly-minded academic divorced from the reality of everyday life. I promise you I am not: I do know the world of work can be a tough place, and I do live in the real world. To show that I have some understanding of what goes on, let me discuss briefly three problems that I discover frequently in organisations (there are many more, of course).

1. TOO MUCH WORK

Pope Benedict XVI attracted widespread press coverage when he cautioned his listeners on the dangers of working too hard. In his address he quoted Bernard of Chiaravelle: "We have to guard ourselves, the saint observed, from the dangers of excessive activity, regardless of the office one holds." The media picked up the pontiff's words with alacrity. It may have been a quiet news month, but the coverage of his words went far beyond the need of some newspaper hack merely to fill some empty column inches. The pope's words had struck a chord with many people—they obviously resonated with people's experiences—and they triggered a sequence of follow-up reports.

One columnist[3] identified the emerging practice in China of providing workers with a mattress for them to take "naps beneath their desks during long working days," of the pressure to relax the requirements of the Working Time Directive in Europe, and of the relative lack of paid holidays in America. Another newspaper commissioned its New York correspondent[4] to examine the reluctance of many US workers to take their holiday entitlement. The newspaper's editorial comment drew attention to the "Blackberry withdrawal" (a reference to the palm-held computer) that many executives felt when made to take a break from work. Not to be outdone by its competitor, the first newspaper picked up the Blackberry theme[5] with their tongue-in-cheek comment that "The Blackberry can be as addictive as hard drugs…," a comment based on research undertaken by Rutgers University in New Jersey. By the time the Sunday newspapers tackled the story, the focus was on people who had dropped out of the rat race and chosen alternative lifestyles. One of the Sunday papers[6] described how an investment banker had turned her back on a promising, high-flying career, and other newspapers told similar tales.

The pope had undoubtedly identified a rich vein of thought that many shared. It concerned the very nature of work and its place within the lives of people. While millions of people across the world need to work but are unable to do so for economic and other reasons, there are many in the rest of the world where work has taken over their lives and made them unaware of, or inured to, the true meaning of life. The long-hours culture has caused harm to the individual and families; and for a generation of children and young people, their experience of family life is often confined to mothers and fathers who are too busy to devote valuable time and who instead lavish gifts on them in attempts to expunge their feelings of guilt.

2. TOO MUCH STRESS

Everyone knows that a certain amount of stress can actually improve performance; it gives that small edge, that adrenalin rush, which is so often needed to perform at one's very best. But too much stress can cause substantial harm to a person's lifestyle and health.

The level of concern regarding stress in the UK has led to the Chartered Institute of Personnel Management (CIPD), the professional body for human resource practitioners, and the Health and Safety Executive (HSE), the government watchdog tasked with policing health and safety issues, to issue a series of guidelines for employers and employees. Employers have become aware of the potential for litigation from those who have become ill as a result of stress caused in their places of work. The CIPD Web site contains a synopsis of recent research[7] and makes alarming reading.

No matter the amount of research, the acid test for most is the level of stress they and their loved ones experience in their daily lives, and the feeling (subjective perhaps) is that things are getting worse rather than better for many.

3. TOO LITTLE DEVELOPMENT

How frustrating it must feel for employees of a company that needs their commitment, knowledge, talent, and skills and yet the organisation does not tap into this intellect and experience to bring out the best they have to offer. Does such a scenario sound far-fetched? Is there any doubt that some companies are run in this way? I present two short pieces of evidence for consideration.

Marcus Buckingham[8] has become well known for his impressive work on the "use your strengths" agenda. In his research he asked the question "What percent of people spend most of the day playing to their strengths?" His results were alarming. In the US the answers were: 2005—17 percent; 2006—14 percent; and 2007—12 percent.

Stephen Covey in his book *The 8th Habit*[9] quotes from the results of a Harris poll of twenty-three thousand US residents. The table of results shows that only 37 percent of respondents believed they had a clear understanding of what their organisation was trying to achieve and why. And the reactions to their team and organisation's goals, their job satisfaction, and views on open communication showed further sources for concern.

Just think about the figures in these examples for a moment. If these were isolated examples they would be more understandable, but these figures resonate across international boundaries and business-sector demarcation lines.

Alongside these three illustrative problems here are two trends that bring encouragement.

1. RECOGNISING POTENTIAL

"Employee engagement," one more buzz phrase in the management community, signifies the drive to engage employees in the aims and values of the organisation, including a willingness to support the efforts of their colleagues. One professional body defined this development as:

> Employers want employees who will do their best work, or "go the extra mile" [and] employees want good work: jobs that are worthwhile and turn them on.... [10]

According to the literature, employers realise that "turned on workers," to use their inelegant descriptor, produce better results, which in turn leads to higher profits, and even the most myopic of employers recognise the intrinsic qualities of a more committed workforce. For many employers, their motives may be driven by "bottom line" arguments, but the change is driven by something far greater—recognition of the concept of intellectual capital.

Thomas A. Stewart, a leading intellectual capital guru, describes perfectly these changes taking place within the employment relationship:

> The rise of the knowledge worker fundamentally alters the nature of work and the agenda of management. Managers are custodians; they protect and care for the assets of a corporation; when the assets are intellectual, the manager's job changes. Knowledge work doesn't happen the way mechanical labour did. [11]

No doubt the story is apocryphal, but the tale of the boss who encouraged younger managers in the company to wear badges claiming "Smarter than my boss!" is the proper spirit of the age. The badge captures the essence of the comments of the legendary Peter Drucker, the management gurus' guru, who commented "Work on the productivity of the knowledge worker has barely begun." It was Drucker's recognition that the age of developing intellectual capital through the knowledge and expertise of the employee is truly upon us.

2. RESPECTING PRINCIPLES

Many of the most popular management books in the last decade suggest that something significant is taking place in company life. A growing awareness of the importance of inner values or principles is taking place. Consider these words from Stephen Covey:

> Something very, very profound is going on....It is a true metamorphosis within our society. I haven't any question about it at all. People have had it with giving their whole lives to a business. I'm sensing a whole lot of imbalance, an awareness of a hollowness in people's lives.[12]

Covey examines the reasons for this and concludes, amongst other things, that: "people are feeling a need for values and principles that don't change."

A growing number of people have become tired of narcissistic approaches to leadership, of leaders who preen themselves and tell the world how good they are. In Jim Collins's book *Good to Great*[13] Collins tells how he and his research team discovered that truly effective executives demonstrate two clusters of leadership attributes: the first set of attributes comes under the heading of "Professional Will" and the second set is most revealing, including terms and key points such as the need for humility, modesty, inspired standards, and recognising the worth of other people.

Bill George was the CEO of Medtronic, a company whose market capitalization increased from $1.1 billion to $60 billion in a twelve-year period, and in *Authentic Leadership* and his later *True North*[14] he addressed the essence of leadership in a business world where the old supposed verities are being challenged. His first book was written as the US began to recover from the shock of Enron, and the book contains thought-provoking challenges such as:

> We need authentic leaders, people of the highest integrity, committed to building enduring organizations. We need leaders who have a deep sense of purpose and are true to their core values.

Peter Block, in *Stewardship,*[15] makes a similar point:

> There resides in each of us the desire to more fully integrate our lives. We must feel fragmented…."This is my work life," "this is my personal life," "this is my spiritual life." In compartmentalizing our lives, we are constantly setting aside parts of ourselves, even at times giving ourselves away.

Ken Blanchard, the author of many best-selling books, including *Managing by Values,*[16] imaginatively and creatively developed the concept of a "Fortunate 500" company ©—a neat play on words. Blanchard contends that:

> Rather than focusing solely on results, winning companies first emphasize values—the beliefs, attitudes, and feelings that top management has about employees, customers, quality, ethics, integrity, social responsibility, growth, stability, innovation, and flexibility.

Danah Zohar, coauthor of *Spiritual Capital,*[17] believes:

> Human beings are essentially spiritual creatures….We are driven, indeed we are defined, by a specifically human longing to find meaning and value in what we do and experience. We have a longing to see our lives in some larger, meaning-giving context….

Zohar goes on to suggest how companies can foster spiritual capital within their organisations with recommendations that include trust, self-awareness, compassion, and a sense of vocation (that is, being called to "serve" something larger than myself). Within a relatively short period of time, organisational spirituality has moved from a rather flaky, fringe agenda to a position where various companies give it serious consideration.

I realise the quotes are brief and from only a small number of references, but these books represent a growing body of literature expressing an emerging awareness of the deeper needs of employees and the organisations in which they work. I believe these to be significant developments, providing opportunities for people who wish to make a difference in their place of work.

Challenge

Whatever your circumstances I hope you see signs that encourage you to make a difference in the world you inhabit. One of Gandhi's most famous sayings, "We must be the change we wish to see in the world," should be your focus. I understand you cannot change the world on your own, perhaps not even your own department, but that does not mean that you cannot make some kind of valuable difference. Gandhi's words invite people to live their lives as they would like others to live theirs. You ask, "Will that make a difference? Can this really be done? Aren't the odds against it overwhelming? Will my small efforts make a difference?" The answer is that your decision to act in a particular way, a way consistent with the principles in this book, can make a difference over time. You might be the first one to act this way in your company, but you will not be alone, as you will join many people across the world who believe that their small actions can lead to consequential benefits for others. What a privilege that is.

The four servant-leadership dimensions in part 2 help you consider and decide how to become the person you ought and hopefully want to be. (For those not familiar with the notion of being a servant-leader, I encourage you to visit the Web sites of the Greenleaf Center for Servant Leadership in Indianapolis or that of Don Frick & Associates, to read Robert K. Greenleaf's *The Servant as Leader*,[18] my earlier book *To Be a Servant-Leader*,[19] or many others on the theme.)

Quite deliberately, I have used the words *consider* and *decide*, as there is no intention on my part to be prescriptive, somehow claiming that what will work for one person will work in exactly the same way for everyone else when, in reality, people are different and face a range of different challenges in very different contexts. The four servant-leadership dimensions are opportunities for reflection as you decide upon the appropriate steps you should take. Part 2 of the book is focused on action, and you will find many ideas to stimulate your thinking as you embark on your journey to *move the cheese*.

While undertaking the research for this book, I was struck time and again by the number of companies who used general phrases such as: "going the extra mile," especially in terms of customer service; "treating others as you want to be treated yourself," with regard to fellow staff; and how these general phrases were developed into specific principles, such as: "…highest standards of ethical conduct in every aspect of their work"; "compassion, integrity, and honesty in all situations, to listen with respect to others and to value differences"; and to "recognize the moral issue." There were further examples, and while these phrases are not the sole prerogative of one view of the world, they are nonetheless compatible with the provenance I use in the next part of the book.[b] For that reason the style of writing varies in some parts of chapters 4 through 7, and on occasions may resemble a set of aphorisms for consideration and application.

You can join a band of people committed to *moving the cheese*.

> Of all the will toward the ideal in mankind only a small part can manifest itself in public action. All the rest of this force must be content with small and obscure deeds. The sum of these, however, is a thousand times stronger than the acts of those who receive wide public recognition. The latter, compared to the former, are like the foam on the waves of a deep ocean.—Albert Schweitzer[c]

---

b. Many of the phrases used by companies are taken from the Bible and are representative of a number of management phrases that are direct quotes or based upon such teaching. Part 2 is based upon such timeless principles.

c. Albert Schweitzer, *Out of My Life and Thought* (New York: New American Library, 1963).

PART 2

THE ROLE OF AN EFFECTIVE SERVANT-LEADER

CHAPTER 4
The Purposeful Leader
··

For some leaders[a] the question can be an agonising one; for others the question never crosses their minds; and for most leaders it is something they give serious consideration to from time to time: how can I perform effectively as a leader and still act in accordance with my personal principles? Or to put it another way: how can I look in the mirror in the morning and feel comfortable that I am acting in line with my innermost beliefs? In more prosaic language the question is: how is it possible to "…live a life worthy of the calling I have received?"[20]

Leaders from all walks of life are becoming aware that there must be more to life than the tangible rewards they receive from work alone. There is something they are missing out on, that extra dimension that gives life its fuller meaning. Perhaps it is a *something* they cannot define, but they know there must be more to life than they are currently experiencing. They want to live a life in line with their fundamental beliefs, one that feeds the hunger felt deep within, and it leads them to ask fundamental questions. These questions are often practical and concern living a life that has a deeper purpose: a life where the *real* them has been discovered and is revealed to the world around them. They want their actions to have a positive effect on the lives of those they influence.

Whatever your role, this chapter will help you become respected for the way you work. It will also help you become a dedicated individual, even if cynics delight in attacking your motives and, above all, it will encourage you to relish the opportunities presented to illumi-

---

a. Although I use the word *leader* in these four dimensions, I do not wish to exclude anyone who would describe him- or herself as a *manager*. Too often the two terms are used to create artificial distinctions.

nate discussions, to develop emerging ideas, and to guide the way that your colleagues examine issues within your organisation. You may even become known for the special contribution you make to the way in which business is conducted.

It is not a person's official job title in life that is the most important thing about them; rather it is how they act—how they conduct themselves in the various duties and occasional trials that are presented. It is on these occasions that the real person can be seen and the biggest opportunities arise to make a contribution to the lives of others.

This chapter is based on sound and long-standing principles. At times it is written in what may appear to be a set of rules, although there are many suggestions on how these rules can be translated into principles and meaningful sets of actions. The numerous reference points for the chapter will help further reflection.

Twelve Evidences of the Purposeful Leader

1. ACTS ETHICALLY AND WITH INTEGRITY

All people and all organisations have values. The acid test is not whether values actually exist but whether those values stand up to close examination, whether the values are good ones or bad ones (and there are many people and many organisations with bad values), and whether the declared values are actually consistent with those being practised. It really is astonishing how often what a leader *says* and what a leader *does* differ considerably, and when behaviour fails to square with principles, then the person making a statement concerning those principles is rightly open to the charge of hypocrisy.

Purposeful leaders do their best to ensure that their conduct is based on truthfulness—colleagues can trust them to tell the truth. They will not lie to their associates, mislead them, or "spin them a yarn" to cause harm. Understandably, there are times when it is difficult to tell the truth, and there are instances when the purposeful leader will have to exercise tact to protect the feelings of the individual or to retain commercial confidentialities, but this should be done without straying into the territory of deliberate lies and falsehoods.

If the purposeful leader shows unjust anger against someone, then they do their best, wherever possible, to mend those broken fences before the end of the day. In that way they restore their sound working relationship with the individual. Also, they do their best to guard the words that come from their mouth in the first place. It is difficult to be seen as an upright individual if one is known for telling cruel jokes or making discriminatory comments about someone else or for commanding a wide range of choice expletives. It is better to be known for saying things that help people, especially people who may need encouragement. The purposeful leader will never speak slanderously about other people and does not join in when someone is being "run down" behind their back. They try to develop attitudes that really want the best for other people.

Leaders live under all sorts of pressure, so purposeful leaders will do their best to maintain a calm disposition: one free from bitterness towards others or bouts of anger, one that makes a point of not acting maliciously towards others, even when wronged and where the temptation to act in a malicious way is almost overwhelming. They try to act in a fair and proper manner towards others.

The purposeful leader will be known as a good listener rather than as a good talker, because good talkers are usually more interested in themselves and what they have achieved than in the achievements or problems of other people. Being measured in speech allows the purposeful leader a greater opportunity to think about what they have to say and to check whether what they are about to say is something to be regretted later. Losing control of one's tongue can result in trouble, and many people live to regret what was said in a hurry—measured thoughts and measured words ought to be the order of the day for everyone. The tongue is a small part of the body, but it can have a devastating effect on relationships and, unfortunately, there are some people who believe it sensible to say whatever comes to mind. "I speak my mind," they claim, but that is rarely a sensible course to take, and it is far wiser to keep one's tongue in check. Without such discipline people are sometimes astonished to discover their tongues praising and cursing the same person. The purposeful leader keeps his or her tongue under control and realises that it is much better to use the tongue to build up people rather than to tear them down.

Purposeful leaders do not let their general behaviour become polluted by the lifestyles of those whose conduct can only be described as suspect: they are the sort of people who decide to pay back a wrong done to them with a greater wrong, or if they are insulted then they hurl back a greater insult. The purposeful leader avoids being influenced by their behaviour and strives to be sympathetic, even compassionate, someone who wants to do the right thing and show respect to other people. Being that sort of person (the latter sort) takes far more courage and earns most people's respect, even if their respect is somewhat grudging.[21]

2. ACCEPTS CHANGE AND RESPECTS DIFFERENCES

Typically, most books on change management concern themselves with the general nature of change, and the process is dealt with predominantly at the level of the organisation or the team. As a result, the one aspect of change not dealt with effectively is what happens when it occurs within an individual. Spencer Johnson's book, however, is a clear exception to this general rule. Individuals can change. There are people who start out implacably opposed to a set of principles, to the chosen strategy of the organisation, and who may even see themselves as the leader of the opposition to a particular chosen way, and then they change their minds. Given the frequency with which management phrases have been lifted from the Bible, it is not too surprising that in many companies such a change of heart by an individual is referred to as "a Damascus Road experience." People do change, they do revise their opinions, and the purposeful leader welcomes those with the courage to change their minds on an issue. These "converts" or "late recruits" can become some of the biggest proponents for their revised approach and can be used in key roles. Initial opposition to an idea should never be held against someone; neither should the early advocates of a new strategy resent the fact that later adherents (a parvenu, for goodness sake!) now take leading roles in making it a success, whereas earlier adherents may adopt lesser roles. Purposeful leaders will encourage an organisational culture that allows people to reassess their position and revise their initial views without any opprobrium being attached to them and without any sense of their being excluded from new developments. All of those involved should have the opportunity to take a fresh look and to change their minds if necessary.

Where the very mission of the organisation needs to be changed, taking a new and perhaps revolutionary look at how things should operate in the future, it is surprising the boundaries people can erect in their minds—imaginary perimeters that limit the scope of vision. They need to be encouraged to take a broader view, not one based on unrealistic dreams about what the company has to offer, but a view free from limitations based on distorted or even selfish restrictions. Companies can now operate in many countries and different environments without even stepping out of their traditional offices, so opportunities for development should never be limited to the paucity of people's imaginations or unrealistic limitations.

Even when change is accepted in principle, coming to terms with its effects can still be challenging. Some people accept change willingly, and others make their opposition known in a considered way, explaining why they do not take the line proposed by others. There is yet another type of person, and they can be the worst person to deal with: in public they accept the proposed changes, but then express their disagreement with complaints behind closed doors.

Favouritism should not be shown towards people because of their status or sociopolitical connections: all people should be treated fairly, realising that everyone has an intrinsic status and worth. There are times when certain people should be honoured for their achievements or because of their position within an organisation, but that is quite different from the general treatment of people on a daily basis. The purposeful leader ensures that ideas are never shelved because of overt or covert prejudice harboured against someone else.

The purposeful leader does things without complaining or arguing. That does not mean that a leader agrees with everything being undertaken. For example, some proposed initiative may be a fundamentally bad management practice or may even be illegal, but the general principle to follow is not to "moan and groan." But being known as someone who doesn't complain makes the purposeful leader's complaints all the more effective if and when they do come.

Because people come from a variety of different backgrounds, belief systems, and cultures, the purposeful leader ensures that everyone is accepted and creates a sense of unity based on the fact that people share a common humanity. Accepting one another and making allowances is an admirable goal, and condescending judgements should never be made towards other people in the workplace. The purposeful leader will see differences as part of a rich kaleidoscope that brings variety to daily lives and encourages people to emphasise elements that join them together and work to bring out the best in one another.[22]

3. COMMITS TO LEARNING AND SELF-DEVELOPMENT

Learning only truly takes place when there is a change of behaviour in an individual or team, and the purposeful leader is committed to his or her own learning, able to reflect on life's experiences, and keen to serve as an example to others.

There are times when the absence of learning is a direct result of a lack of application by individuals who seem to be incapable of learning from formal knowledge sources and cannot reflect on the experiences of life. This is so unfortunate for the individual and also a critical factor for the company and its development. Where effective learning mechanisms are in place the individual needs to be encouraged to take part. No one should be expected to become an accomplished learner immediately, but everyone should be expected to achieve this goal over time. One of the best ways of achieving this is to act sequentially: to become a progressive learner by taking small steps to move from one stage to another. This stepping-stone approach means that the learner can move from one degree of learning to another through small steps, learning more and more as they make progress.

Team learning takes place best when team members are prepared to discuss successes and failures and learn lessons from them. Where teams are able to turn their collective thinking and energy into something greater than the sum of their individual parts, it means that their thinking and learning have "come alive." As a result they are able to develop as individuals and as a group. To belong to a team that achieves more than others thought they would as a result of meaningful learning translated into action can be one of the most rewarding experiences for the purposeful leader.[23]

4. SHOWS HUMILITY

Humility is the most attractive of qualities; humble people are a joy to be with, while proud people extract a considerable amount of patience and goodwill from those who have to endure their company. Proud people seek every opportunity to tell others about their achievements and are likely to exaggerate what they have accomplished. Like proud peacocks, they puff out their chests in an ugly display of self-aggrandisement. They are so absorbed with what *they* have done that when someone else is speaking there is little attempt to listen: for them, it is all about me, me, me, and they have scant interest in the lives of others. Proud people even avoid those occasions that offer little opportunity to preen themselves in public or to add to what they consider to be their growing band of admirers. They are unpleasant people.

Humble people are the complete opposite. There is pleasure being in their company because they are interested in other people, they don't try to create opportunities to speak about their latest exploits, and they are usually generous of spirit. There are times when their self-effacing approach to life can be overdone, when they go to unreasonable lengths to conceal their accomplishments, but that is to be preferred much more than the antics of proud people. When humble people are invited to a meeting they choose to sit in less conspicuous seats so as not to draw attention to themselves, unlike proud people who seek out a position of power (in their eyes). Humble people would much rather be judged for the quality and helpfulness of their contribution rather than the position of their chair!

The purposeful and humble leader realises it is unnecessary to conform to the ultimately pointless patterns and rituals of the world around them, where people habitually seek recognition; rather they devote themselves to more profitable pursuits that bring better and longer-term rewards. They do not think of themselves as possessing qualities that make them more important than other people, and their estimation of themselves is sober, based on standards much higher than those employed by proud people. They also ensure that their behaviour is not motivated by selfish ambition or by what can be termed vain conceit. They are happy to be in a position where they are ready and willing to praise the efforts of others and are not afraid to speak of those efforts as better than their own. How refreshing it is to be in their presence.[24]

5. VALUES HARD WORK AND DEPENDABILITY

Cynics will refer sneeringly to someone as having a "work ethic." This may mean that the cynic does not understand the supposed traditions and respective views of work and is unlikely to be appreciative of Max Weber's *The Protestant Ethic and the Spirit of Capitalism*. Usually cynics use the phrase as a common cliché, to castigate those who are hardworking, committed to their careers, and focused on the objectives of their companies. In the eyes of sneering cynics hard work has become a sin and the habitat of those who cannot achieve an easy life with substantial amounts of leisure time. The phrase, in other words, has become a slur on the habits of hardworking people.

Purposeful leaders regard hard working as a virtue, not a sin, and diligently undertake their various commitments, thus showing respect to those who have entrusted them with responsibility. They want to be seen as good employees, wholehearted in what they do, and they will try their utmost to lead others effectively, undertaking their leadership responsibilities to the best of their abilities.

The word *discipline* conjures up the most unpleasant consequences in the minds of those who do not conform to a particular set of instructions. Yet discipline, in the punitive sense of the word, is often the last resort, and the word should be understood as having far more to do with training and being dedicated to an ordered life. Being disciplined means knowing how things should be done and being committed to acting in accordance with those standards. At first, it may not feel like a comfortable way to live, especially since some people seem to have been conditioned to an ill-disciplined lifestyle. However, when discipline becomes a habit, it can be a pleasant feature of life and one that produces many benefits.

Inevitably, the word *idle* has to be used to describe some people, even after making charitable allowances for them and the circumstances in which they find themselves. It is not that they cannot work, through illness, disability, or some genuine misfortune; it is just that they will not work—in other words they are bone idle. A point in time may well arrive when the purposeful leader will need to keep some distance from such a person, as they will try and take advantage of the leader's good nature. Some idle people can become busybodies—"the devil makes work for idle hands," as the saying goes—and they involve themselves in issues that don't concern them. Acting properly towards such people is difficult: they should not be treated with hostility, but the purposeful leader should be free to express the view that work, rather than idleness, is right and proper.

Another dimension of discipline is summed up in the word *stickability*—being the type of person who is able to stay with a cause even when the going gets tough and when others may make their excuses and leave. Most individuals and companies experience difficult times, when the prevailing conditions appear to be going against them, and it is at times like these that people need to know who is with them and who is likely to jump ship in search of calmer waters. Many will find the going too difficult and complain about it, but those who stay with the company through "thick and thin," where they are able to do so, are worthy of praise and honour when and if the difficult times have been overcome.

Depending on which reference books are consulted, it was either Gary Player or Arnold Palmer who first said, "The more I practice the luckier I get." Whichever one of the golfing legends first spoke those words, the sentiment resonates with many people: the greatest opportunities in life usually come to those who are prepared to put in the hard work; reward does not come without dedication; and there is something intrinsically rewarding about hard work in and of itself.[b] [(25)]

---

b. Nothing in this section should be taken to mean that I do not believe in leisure time, especially when spent with one's family, or that I do not value what is now termed as a work-life balance.

6. TRIES NOT TO WORRY

Mark Twain was absolutely right: "I have spent most of my life worrying about things that never happened." Most people know that to be true, but they also know that it is very difficult to break the habit of a lifetime.

The purposeful leader understands that worrying is bad for one's health. It is likely to increase blood pressure, cause loss of sleep, lead to a deterioration in performance. These in turn may contribute to fears becoming a reality: the fear of redundancy or being over-looked for promotion may become more likely. Worry is a real factor in many people's lives and is caused, by and large, by the stresses and strains of the world in which they live. Purposeful leaders do their best to ameliorate the stresses and strains that employees experience, and in so doing they release people from unnecessary burdens, allow-ing them to perform to their full potential.[26]

Some bosses (I refuse to call them leaders) deliberately impose worry and anxiety on their people to demonstrate the power and control they have over those under their command. Manfred Kets de Vries, in his fascinating book *The Leader on the Couch—A Clinical Approach to Changing People and Organizations*,[27] introduces his readers to a series of different leadership types based on his assess-ment of personality. One of these types is "the abrasive disposition." He starts with the assertion that many managers today subscribe to the Heinrich Himmler school of management in that they too believe: "Men may hate us. But we don't ask for their love: only for their fear." He shows how people with abrasive dispositions are, inter alia, strongly opinionated, authoritarian, intolerant, harsh, domi-neering, quick to take offence, and he goes on to contend that "...a focus on results becomes an excuse for hostile, hurtful actions...[where]...[the] feelings of others...can't be allowed to interfere with the accomplishment of their goals."

Such bosses are to be deprecated, to use the strongest term, for treating fellow human beings and colleagues so abysmally. How pathetic when a senior manager gets some kick out of being able to impose uncertainty and apprehension upon others within their department—such people exist, and they really are poor specimens of the management profession.

7. BECOMES "SALT" AND "LIGHT"

Many years ago, I worked in a management college, and every four weeks thirty to forty managers would arrive at the college for one of our leadership development programmes. Over the five years I worked there I met and taught hundreds, if not thousands, of managers from across the UK and some from overseas. After I had been in the college for about six months I began to notice that most of the courses seemed to have a distinctive nature or atmosphere and that this difference was influenced by no more than three or four of the course delegates. Some participants were harder working than others, some were serious-minded, and others were full of laughter. Some believed in the maxim of working hard and playing hard—and they played hard in the pubs of the local village. It seemed that no one course was like another. As college staff we treated all course delegates in much the same way, and we were aware of the influence certain people could have on the courses, but no matter what influence we exerted (and, in truth, it was a minimal influence, as these were grown men and women), the style of the course was dictated by and large by the personality of a small number of the course delegates. How interesting to think about this observation when considering the scope for purposeful leaders to be "salt" and "light" within their own companies.

In the world prior to the development of modern techniques, salt was often associated with three quite specific qualities.[c] First, it was related to purity; second, it was used as a preservative, to stop things "going bad"; and third, salt was employed to bring out or add flavour to the food. No wonder people are referred to as being "like the salt of the earth" for their contribution to the lives of others. This is the principal challenge for purposeful leaders: they should be salt within their companies, people who stand for the highest standards of conduct. One does not have to think too long to bring to mind examples where individuals, and even whole businesses, have been

---

c. My thoughts on this and the immediate paragraphs would have been limited without the invaluable guidance of William Barclay—please see references.

associated with low standards of practice, including straightforward dishonesty, where long-standing principles have been ignored.

To be salt, a purposeful leader stands for the best of standards, those that are open to public scrutiny, keeping a company free from the putrefying effects of corruption or general decay, flavouring the very atmosphere of their organisation. In the same way that food without salt lacks its proper taste, so an organisation without its moral compass lacks a major component: it will lose its focus and will eventually lose its way, especially when entering uncharted waters.

Similarly, the purposeful leader will be *light* within the company. The first function of a light is to be seen, as a concealed light will leave a room in darkness; second, a light can act as a guide illuminating the way ahead; third, a light can act as a means of warning, just as a flashing light or a red light at a road junction can warn someone of danger ahead. In these three ways, purposeful leaders can act as sources of light within their companies, making the road ahead clear for others; suggesting that a course of action will move people from light into darkness; providing a lead for others to follow; warning others of the consequences of certain actions; and showing others the incontrovertible benefits of actions open to independent scrutiny.[28]

8. GOES THE EXTRA MILE

In my research for this book I came across the phrase "going the extra mile" repeatedly. Usually, it described the company's customer service policy—"going the extra mile for our customers"—but it was also used in other contexts, such as to describe the ideal relationship between the employer and the employee. The phrase describes a task being done in such a way as to surpass the expectations of the recipient, for example, giving exceptional customer service or undertaking responsibilities in a way that speaks more of the needs of other people than your own.

I can remember arriving in Washington DC one hot summer's afternoon. We had been on a long journey, and after booking into our Georgetown hotel we needed a drink. I asked for a cold bottle of beer and was told that the hotel's refrigerator, holding its bottled drinks, had broken down. I asked for a can of Coke instead and was surprised to see the young waiter run across the road. Moments later he returned with a cold bottle of beer—he had gone to a shop across the road to buy me a beer. What service! How extraordinary, and I shall never forget that example of someone being willing to go the extra mile for a semi-dehydrated Brit. Alternatively, a person can do the absolute minimum and nothing more while giving the impression that even minimal effort is done grudgingly.

The purposeful leader gladly provides service for the benefit of the person receiving it, realising that it is possible to perform tasks better than the standard expected, thus delighting the customer; it is on such principles that the success of many enterprises has been founded. What a delight it is for a customer, employer, or employee when they receive excellent service, one that surpasses their expectations.[29]

9. ACTS MAGNANIMOUSLY

The anonymous author of the saying "Revenge is a dish best eaten cold" was absolutely right in the minds of many people. This is the code by which they live their lives: if someone does them wrong then they will get them back, whatever it takes and no matter how long it takes. In fact, the longer it takes—the colder the dish—the more satisfaction they will get from the plotting, scheming, anticipation, and then execution of their revenge.

I once had the misfortune to work with a manager who possessed a small black book. In this book were written the names of all those people who had crossed the manager and who, one day, would be targeted for "revenge." Names were recorded meticulously, and one by one each downfall was plotted. How tragic! What a ghastly and appalling way to lead one's life! People who behave in such a way will try to justify their actions by phrases such as "Nobody messes with me and gets away with it," and somehow they believe that their trite phrases justify their boorish behaviour.

A different approach exists, one that is based on what writers such as Charles Handy in his masterpiece *Age of Unreason*[30] call "upside down thinking." In the context of being magnanimous, "upside down thinking" means looking at things the wrong way round according to convention. It means not gaining revenge on someone who has wronged you and may mean going further and being kind to those who have acted spitefully towards you. Such an approach does work, not in every instance it has to be said, but at the very least it will make purposeful leaders feel they have taken the moral high ground. They have not returned evil with evil; they have turned the other cheek and have employed a mature reaction to the infantile attacks of lesser people.

A true story illustrates this point. Carol (not her real name) was the CEO of a medium-size company and had risen to the top job on the basis of her expertise, experience, and the toughness and courage that she displayed when faced with serious business challenges. Commendable characteristics, to be sure, but there was a chink in Carol's armour. She treated every problem in exactly the same way. If people disagreed with her, she would treat them as "opponents" and would immediately try to build cases against them. All who disagreed with her were her opponents. In the face of any "opposition," she would never waiver from her prepared arguments and would regularly call in the lawyers to help pressure those who disagreed with her. On one occasion she took unreasonable action against one of her colleagues, but the person did not react with hostility, as Carol had come to expect. The colleague graciously reiterated that she did not agree with Carol, but she did not make too big a deal out of the disagreement. Carol was flummoxed. Her whole "counterattack" against this perceived opponent collapsed. "Upside down thinking" had got the better of her. That was not the reason why it had been practised—her colleague had acted in that manner because it was the right thing to do—but it demonstrated unexpected magnanimity. It would be naïve to suggest that a response similar to Carol's happens in each and every instance and there will be times, of course, when it is right and proper to take action against an individual. These matters have to be judged carefully, but as a general principle magnanimity has much to commend it.

From time to time, events take place between a purposeful leader and someone reporting to them where it is necessary to speak to the individual about their behaviour and to point out that such conduct is considered inappropriate. Unfortunately, following these discussions some people do not change their behaviour, and there may be need to speak with them again, this time in the presence of other people, and if that does not change their behaviour, then the leader may have to consider their future employment with the company. That really should be a last resort, and it is worth investigating whether a magnanimous approach would have an impact in transforming the individual's behaviour, although being committed to the principle of magnanimity should never mean that an unscrupulous individual could take advantage of the goodwill of the purposeful leader.

There is another reason for being magnanimous. When leaders judge others, especially when they are judged against standards the leaders rarely use personally, leaders run the risk of criticising the "specks of dust" in other people's eyes while ignoring the "planks of wood" in their own. It is far better for the leader to show understanding in comments regarding other people, as then it is easier to explain times when leaders are less judgmental about their own inadequacies.[31]

10. PREVENTS AND RESOLVES CONFLICT

Conflict exists within companies for a multitude of reasons, usually involving different views on how or when to achieve common and agreed objectives. Within the senior management team, this can arise over the principal needs of the company at a point in time, or as a result of different personalities, experiences, and cultures that have brought each of the team members to their present position. They may well be united in purpose, but there are tensions in their ranks about the execution of various actions.

At other times, leaders may disagree over the people they wish to deploy to meet challenges or special initiatives that lie ahead. One senior manager believes that a certain individual should be included in the team and another senior manager does not; the second manager may doubt whether the person can be relied upon when the going gets tough. In these circumstances, and especially if the individual at the centre of the disagreement is a relative of one of the managers, there may be an element of division in the senior management ranks, with both managers forming teams wishing to set off in different directions. This is unhelpful, to say the least, and the purposeful leader will need to resolve such tensions, and there are times when it is best to have the two "opponents" work in different areas for the time being. The fact remains that both senior managers are totally committed to the same overall purposes of the company, but the sharp words they have exchanged may mean that reconciliation will need to come later.

Conflict may even arise when staff in the company have a preference to work on one leader's team more than another's, tacitly expressing a preference for one leader over another equally senior person. This can happen for many reasons: one leader may be seen as more charismatic, or as more of a people person than the other leader, or it may be the nature or location of the work. Whatever the reason, the purposeful leader will stress the importance of the overall purpose of the company or the individual project in question, and will also emphasise that it is essential for people to work in areas where their talents can be used best, wherever practicable.

Conflict can also arise over what can only be described as stupid and foolish arguments concerning relatively trivial matters, and the purposeful leader avoids such meaningless encounters. However, there may be occasions when the leader is dragged into such disagreements, and the best course of action in these circumstances is to extricate oneself as quickly as possible and ensure that steps are taken to prevent any feelings of resentment as a result of the dispute and any unhelpful comments that were made. Hopefully, the people involved in the verbal fisticuffs will discover a better way to behave and will learn eventually to behave more responsibly and maturely.

Unfortunately, there will be times when the purposeful leader comes across as thoroughly unpleasant and potentially destructive to people in the company. There are people who desire positions of authority that they do not deserve; they love to be first in everything: the first in a queue, the first to speak, the first to be thanked, and they do all of this to feed the unrealistic ambition that drives their very existence. In an attempt to be seen as the number one person, they undermine those in authority within the company and sometimes do this by spreading malicious gossip to spoil the person's reputation and enhance their own. Additionally, they may attempt to prevent visits to the company from senior people who will see through their Machiavellian scheming. Such unruly and disruptive people have to be tackled head on and cannot be allowed to cause disruption within the company, and it is even likely that they will have to be "shown the door," as that is the only message they understand clearly.

Some other people, who also wish to undermine the company's leader, adopt far subtler methods in an attempt to achieve their goals: they reject authority, but in a way not easy to detect. They are likely to speak abusively about company policies—often when they do not appreciate the reasons for the policy—and they are a decidedly bad influence in the company. They may try to take advantage of more reasonable and measured people, they grumble about each new initiative, find fault with just about every existing practice, boast about their own so-called achievements, attempt to flatter other employees in order to recruit them to their distorted view of the world, and suggest that the company, or a particular venture within the company, should be run according to their plans. Where such men and women exist they need to be found and removed from the organisation. There is no other option, and for this reason alone it is essential to have sophisticated recruitment and performance methods in place. Fortunately, such people are rare, but an encounter with them can be an unpleasant experience.

The vast majority of people prefer to work for a company where there is unity of purpose and where people act reasonably and do their best to get along well with their colleagues and others. They prefer peace to conflict and generally avoid any attempt at cunning to achieve goals. They are willing to express their opinion on issues being raised, and may at times disagree with a given view or suggest an alternative direction for the business, but they have learned to do so in a constructive way, indicating that they wish the company to prosper for the benefit of all concerned. They realise that all the people in the company have similar interests, and they remain committed to one another.

It is such a blessing to have people who are wise in the ways they conduct themselves and who show that their knowledge and understanding of issues are based on their experience of how things should be done. They are the people who set standards within the company;

they live lives that can be described as examples to others. Through their disposition they show that there is an ethical and professional manner in which to conduct one's business. For them there is no question of selfish ambition, and they are genuinely pleased by the success of other people, in seeing others prosper. They develop sound relationships, and their influence can be felt throughout the whole company. They are major assets, and the purposeful leader treasures their contribution.[32]

11. MAKES USE OF GIFTS

It is one thing to have a number of gifts, but it is quite another thing to make use of them. Often gifts are hidden away, or they may have grown rusty through lack of use, or it may be that the person has not realised that he or she has such a gift. Even if it is not a major gift, it is still a gift, and it needs to be used for the benefit of one and all. It is helpful to think that any gift has been given to an individual for a purpose and that it needs to be used for the benefit of others in the company and the wider community.

Purposeful leaders should be able to identify the unique gifts that others possess. One employee may be an expert at planning events or meetings. Another may have a gift for developing strategies for accomplishing future goals. Another person may be skilled at encouraging coworkers to do their best or at perceiving when a coworker needs a word of encouragement. Some people may not be the first to get bright ideas for the company, but they may be superb team players, actively serving the needs of everyone in the group. Still other employees may have the gift of teaching and instructing. Some people are excellent observers of what takes place in the company and can evaluate projects for the future benefit of their companies. For you, the purposeful leader, the best way to serve fellow employees is by exercising appropriate leadership.[33]

12. DOES GOOD: INVESTING IN PEOPLE AND CAUSES

A purposeful leader may never become an Andrew Carnegie, who gave away $4.3 billion (2005 figures) to a variety of foundations and charities during his life, or a Bill Gates, who has donated many billions of dollars to various charitable causes through the Bill and Melinda Gates Foundation; but a purposeful leader can make a difference. As we saw in chapter 2, many companies and individuals make significant contributions through charitable and social activities—one of the key people propositions that differentiates those companies. This has an important effect on the contributor and the people within the company, with most people feeling gratified that attempts are made to help others.

As opportunities to help people arise, it is unfortunate that some leaders take a narrow view of giving their time and resources. The purposeful leader will be seen as someone who is prepared to be generous with time and resources and who is willing to contribute meaningfully to the needs of others. Many opportunities for involvement exist, and they can be matched to meet available time and to ensure that skills and resources are used optimally. Purposeful leaders believe that being involved in the needs of other people is good for business as well as for those who benefit from the contribution. It is not that involvement is calculated on a mercenary basis, as if there were an exact calculation of the financial return to the business, but rather, purposeful leaders believe there to be long-term advantages that come from an enhanced reputation for the company, from increased staff satisfaction, and from a general sense of well-being. They believe that they get back more than they put in, and leaders understand that the return is often not subject to strict financial analysis.[34]

Conclusion

The old, scripturally derived saying "No prophet is accepted in the prophet's home town" is alive and kicking in the twenty-first century, and those working for a purposeful leader may be among the last people to acknowledge their leader's valuable contribution. Purposeful leaders should not despair, as outside their companies there will be people who recognise what they are accomplishing. By means of networks, purposeful leaders can learn about one another and join ranks, and these rewarding and stimulating associations will provide the strength needed to carry on during challenging times. The camaraderie of other purposeful leaders sharing a similar set of principles will prove to be a motivating force.

Inevitably, there will be times when purposeful leaders feel that they have acted in contravention of their principles: that they have been a failure—not to put too fine a point on it. There will be a feeling of letting others down and of being open to the charge of being no more than a hypocrite. Some colleagues will point an accusing finger and suggest that, like everyone else, the purposeful leader has denied the very things that they claimed to stand for. This can be a difficult experience. Also, there will be times when the purposeful leader feels trapped, cornered on all sides, and that the only way to act is in a fashion that lies outside one's normal style. These are difficult moments, yet they are a common experience, and the only solution is to do whatever one can do, to act as best as one can within the circumstances and to realise that most people will empathise and appreciate the difficult circumstances that had to be manoeuvred.

All of this is not easy. On occasions, the decision to act as a purposeful leader will cause discouragement, and the decision to occupy the moral higher ground will be seen as some sort of failure. At times like this it is understandable to cry out, "Don't they realise that I am not taking the easy route; I have decided to act honourably?" Often, the purposeful leadership will not be recognised, perhaps for many years, but recognition usually does come, and there will be an opportunity for people to acknowledge the admirable way in which leadership was exercised. The key question is whether to behave with an eye on short-term popularity or longer-term recognition by those whose judgement is truly valuable.[35]

Being a purposeful leader is a fundamental component in *moving the cheese* for the benefit of others.

Preach the Gospel always, and when necessary use words.
—St. Francis of Assisi

Summary—The Purposeful Leader:

1. Acts ethically and with integrity.
2. Accepts change and respects differences.
3. Commits to learning and self-development.
4. Shows humility.
5. Values hard work and dependability.
6. Tries not to worry.
7. Becomes "salt" and "light."
8. Goes the extra mile.
9. Acts magnanimously.
10. Prevents and resolves conflict.
11. Makes use of gifts.
12. Does good: investing in people and causes.

CHAPTER 5
The Principled Leader

•••

Storytelling is gaining ground in academic circles as a legitimate means to understand organisations, the people within them, and the environment in which they operate, as this quote from Harvard professor Rosabeth Moss Kanter illustrates:

> I think that people learn best through stories....I believe that the most useful ideas are grounded in a deep understanding of how the world actually works. That is why I value getting out in the field, talking with people in their own settings.[36]

What follows is a collection of sixteen leadership principles based on stories of everyday life from long ago, and the themes within these stories contain a significant message for the leader of today—for the person I have called the principled leader. On occasions, the old stories have inspired some modern-day storytelling to develop a particular principle further.

1. ESTABLISHES SOLID FOUNDATIONS

This is a simple yet profound principle: it is essential to have in place solid foundations to underpin each main individual and corporate activity; otherwise various calamities will afflict a person's career and organisation. If someone fails to have such foundations, if the basis of their working life has been built on a substance as unstable as sand rather than rock, then it is likely that they will experience the equivalent of the climatic extremes of monsoon rain, floods, and winds beating ferociously against them, and the likelihood of everything they have built crumbling and falling in ruins around their feet. Not a very pleasant experience, to be sure.

The principled leader is much wiser and makes certain to put in place solid foundations; foolhardy people decide to gamble—to take a risk and to put it off until another day—and are far more likely to see everything come tumbling down around their feet. Developing solid foundations is essential, whether they be known as ethics or sound financial procedures or whatever. Without such firm foundations to guide what individuals and companies set out to achieve, it is likely that they will be like someone tossed about by gusts of wind or tremors of the ground beneath their feet.[37]

As I put the finishing touches to this text (in September 2008), the words above have a particular poignancy in the light of environmental threats that have seen hurricanes lashing many coastlines and financial threats that led to the collapse of supposedly established financial institutions. This first principle is not meant as a critique of any country or individual company, nor of environmental policies and business practice, but the dramatic events do underscore the significance and importance of this first tenet of the principled leader.

2. KNOWS THEIR PEOPLE

When a principled leader launches an initiative within the company, he or she is not surprised to discover various reactions from four different types of people: those who are difficult to convince about anything; those who may be convinced at the superficial level but who lack commitment to back up their initial agreement; those who are convinced by the merits of the argument but who become easily distracted by some new fad or another latest exciting development; and those who understand what the principled leader is trying to achieve and become wholeheartedly committed to the initiative set out before them. Four different types of people requiring four quite different strategies.

Those who are difficult to convince about anything are likely to react to all new ideas in a negative manner, and they are likely to be the sort of people who possess closed minds. They are hard to convince, not open to new ideas, resist the prospect of change, and typically are not prepared to assess present conditions and the need for change. Attempting to convince such people about most things is a fruitless and pointless exercise: their minds closed—closed tight, as tight as a clam. They carry around with them their set of favourite prejudices and, no matter what they claim, they do not wish to be taught anything remotely new or revolutionary. Sometimes, and for quite irrational reasons, they will resent the principled leader and his or her new ideas and no amount of reasoning will make them change their minds.

The person who may be convinced at the superficial level but who lacks commitment to back up their initial agreement may be enthusiastic initially to the principled leader's ideas, but clearly has not thought through the implications of such a positive response. They love each new initiative, give it their full support, say how much they want to be involved, talk of little else (especially if it makes them appear positive in front of their boss), but are likely to abandon the new initiative as quickly as they adopted the idea, to go chasing after the latest next new initiative. It is likely that their response was merely at the emotional level, without much thought given to the consequences and obligations, and any true commitment sought from them is unlikely to be forthcoming.

Others, and these are a variation or combination of types 2 and 3 people, are well and truly signed up to the new initiative—they really are genuine—but they are so busy with many other activities and genuine commitments that they cannot give the time to make the new idea a reality. They are terribly apologetic—"If there's anything I can do please let me know"—and they mean it, but they are far too busy to get involved in anything that will help take the new ideas forward. They suffer from one of the curses of modern life: their lives are becoming busier and busier, and more and more complex; undoubtedly they are genuine people, but just too busy to get to grips with essential priorities.

Finally, there are people who are truly interested in the new ideas and can be relied upon to see things through to the end. They have open minds and are willing to learn. They are certainly not too busy to ask searching diagnostic questions and not too proud to admit when they do not know the answers. Before committing to the principled leader's plans they have thought things through and are prepared to accept the inevitable challenges, and it is evident that they are likely to be ideal allies in what needs to be achieved.

When faced with these four types of people, there are choices to be made. Should the principled leader risk wasting time casting the seed of good ideas far and wide and engaging in countless debates with people whose minds are closed and who are incapable of, or unwilling to engage in, objective thought? Or, should the principled leader spend time with shallow people, people who have little depth to their thinking, trying to cultivate those whose response to most things is enthusiastic but display little prospect of significant yet alone substantial participation in the advance of progress? How should the principled leader react to those who will pull out at the last moment, to those busy people who cannot make meetings or fail to live up to commitments? Should the principled leader only engage with those people who are prepared to commit to new initiatives and who will stand by the leader throughout the journey?

In an ideal world the principled leader would be able to choose the fourth option and exclude the former three from any plans, but in the real world there may be a need to deal with all four types. At least it is advantageous to be able to distinguish the four reactions that may be encountered and to decide how to react to them.[38]

3. FINDS THE RIGHT LEVERS

Small changes and tiny interventions can lead to dramatic changes in the status quo. If a seemingly inconsequential mustard seed can produce the largest of garden plants and become a tree to provide comfort and protection for birds, and a small amount of yeast can "come to life" and contribute to producing sustenance for many, then the potency of small changes made in the business world should never be underestimated.

Management textbooks sometimes quote the Greek mathematician and engineer Archimedes, who lived almost three hundred years BC and identified (amongst many other things) the utility of the lever and the significance of the fulcrum, and condense much of his work into the useful and challenging phrase, "Give me a lever and I can move the world." Similarly, these textbooks often quote what is commonly known as the "butterfly effect"—that concept in chaos theory demonstrating that a small variation in one part of the overall system, the equivalent of the butterfly flapping its wings in a remote jungle, can cause substantial changes in the eventual behaviour of the global or corporate system.

The science lying behind these two concepts is not the principal concern; the main issue is that commentators on business practice realise that introducing small changes into structures and processes can lead to substantial changes in the company at some future stage, and can even effect changes within different parts of the greater overall system. The leadership challenge is to discover those small key changes or, in the absence of that certainty, to be willing to consider experimenting with small changes to a number of variables, as often the answer to current and future problems and the creation of potential major opportunities lie in taking small steps rather than in laying down large and grandiose plans.

When the principled leaders discover small changes that bring rich rewards, they invest heavily in these concepts, do their very best to make them work, and stick with them over considerable periods of time. Often there is agreement on what has to be done, and considerable excitement generated by the potential of the idea, but the initial enthusiasm wanes within quite a short period of time, as other pressures are encountered or as other opportunities occur. The principled leader believes it to be important to stay with excellent ideas, to pursue all the opportunities they present, and to ensure that ideas are valued so that the organisation maximises the full benefits.

Many companies ensure that they have in place systems to encourage the identification and promotion of new ideas (see, for example, the story of 3M in chapter 2), as they realise that from small acorns large oaks grow or, in the context of this chapter, out of seeds as small as the mustard seed large growth can be experienced for the benefit of one and all.[39]

4. CREATES FRIENDSHIPS

Everybody needs friends: people they can rely on, those they can trust, people whom they know will have their best interests at heart.

Friends can meet a variety of needs: through social contact with them and their families, they afford us the chance to relax and enjoy the companionship of other people, and help us celebrate family events and anniversaries. They can also offer support during difficult times within the family or at work, or when there are particular and tangible needs.

Being a leader can be a lonely existence, especially if they are one of the few senior people in the company, so having a network of friends to offer support is important. Having friends within the place of work who can be asked for advice or trusted to give an honest opinion is an added bonus. At times, the principled leader will need someone to talk to, and in extreme circumstances to "pour out one's heart," to explain how difficult life is at present. On the positive side, there will be many occasions when family and personal successes can be celebrated with friends who genuinely enter the spirit of festivity. The company and wisdom of friends are invaluable.

Some people find it difficult to make and maintain friendships. It may be a feature of their personality type, or because they have been encouraged to develop an independent streak—standing on their own two feet and not relying on others for support. Or possibly the hectic pace of life leaves little room to create friendships, or once they had a friend who let them down badly, resulting in a vow never to get close to another person: it may be a case of "once bitten and twice shy."

The principled leader needs friends, and if there is an absence of friends for whatever reason, then there is a need to cultivate a network. Those with various networks of friends tell how easy it is to neglect them. Again, despite the pace and complexity of everyday life, it is important to meet friends regularly, to talk about a variety of different things—family, sport, holiday plans, and much else, but not work if at all possible. Friends can serve as a barometer to indicate the really important things taking place in life (and that may include work); without their advice and counsel the principled leader is a far poorer person.

Friends should be bold with one another. This does not mean taking unfair advantage of one another, but it does mean taking full advantage of the benefits friends are willing to give, and when friends offer advice it is foolish to ignore their collective wisdom.[40]

5. UTILISES TALENTS

One of the saddest things to observe is the way in which some people's talents are wasted in an organisation. Their talents remain undiscovered, and even when they are discovered, they are often underutilised or ignored completely (as shown in chapter 3).

It is all too easy to lay the blame for this misuse of talents wholly at the door of the leaders of the company when, in truth, it is also the responsibility of the individual to make the best use of his or her talents. A person should not sit down passively, waiting for someone who will come along, discover their talents, and then call upon them for help; but that is just what many people do. There is a need for an active response from the individual but, unfortunately, some people are content to keep things exactly as they are; they fail to see the opportunities that are available, they lack adventure, and they and their companies end up as the losers.

Conversely, it is a pleasure to meet people who realise that they and others will benefit from making the most of what they have been given. They seize opportunities to put their talents to work; they believe that they have certain God-given talents (a literal belief for some and a metaphorical one for others), and they are determined to make the most of them. Many believe that talent is like a human muscle, and if they develop this "talent muscle" it will grow and become stronger, and if they fail to develop it then the talent is likely to waste away—just as a muscle can atrophy. There appears to be a general rule in this: when a person uses the talents given to them, then those talents will grow, but if they do nothing with their talents, they will diminish and may disappear over time.

Most people have at least one talent, so do not listen sympathetically to the unduly humble person who claims to have no talent at all. Some may have as many as five talents, and there are those who are fortunate enough to have ten or more talents. The significant point is not the amount of talents they have been given but the key is whether they use those talents fully and properly for the benefit of others and themselves.

There are limits around the acquisition of talents—for example, no matter how much a person practices they will never play golf like

Tiger Woods or tennis like Roger Federer unless they are similarly talented—but that does not mean that it is not possible to acquire additional skills. For example, it is ridiculous for a person to claim they cannot undertake a necessary task when a short training course would remedy that deficiency. They should always be prepared to develop skills to meet the needs of changing circumstances and to accept new opportunities.[a]

One of the ironies concerning the use of talents is that when people use their talents it is likely that the result will be the allocation of larger tasks and greater responsibilities. They may be familiar with the saying that suggests that those who have much will be given even more and that more will be asked of those who are already contributing much already. This appears to be another one of life's general rules and may seem unfair to some, but to others it is a perfectly reasonable way to proceed and is a far better option than to be the person with one talent who simply does not use that talent and allows it to become dormant and therefore pointless.[41]

6. PRACTISES STEWARDSHIP

How marvellous when people realise the true worth of something, be it property, finances or, and most importantly of all, people. When someone understands the true worth of something and not just its financial cost, then they realise that it is essential and intrinsically rewarding to take the utmost care of that asset.

Some people take a cavalier approach to their organisation's assets: "I've only lost one of them, there's still ninety-nine left"; "Only a few pounds/dollars have gone missing, let's enjoy spending the rest of the money"; and most tragically of all, "One of my closest colleagues may have 'gone off the rails' but, what the heck, there's work to be done—let's get on with it." Such attitudes are all too common, and often people attempt to legitimise their responses with phrases such as: "Well, life must go on" or "You win some, you lose some" or "It's no use crying over spilt milk" or "Life's too short to worry about that" or "There's plenty more where that came from."

---

a. I appreciate that I have drifted away from talents to say something concerning the acquisition of skills.

Those attitudes are unacceptable when it comes to the physical resources within the company—people need to be taught the benefits of sound stewardship of one's resources and of good husbandry—but when the same attitude is shown towards people, who have become "lost" in some way, then this attitude is dreadful. Unfortunately, some managers see the people within the organisation as just another resource they have to manage, in much the same way as any other product or raw material.

That is why it is so encouraging to read of the growing band of companies, led by principled leaders, who realise the true worth of their people, who treat them with the dignity and the respect they deserve, and genuinely want their people to develop. These enlightened employers also appreciate that there are times when things can go wrong in a person's life. An individual may make an incorrect decision, believing that somehow "the grass will be greener in another field," only to realise that the "grass" is actually inferior to what has been left behind. In circumstances such as this the attitude displayed by former colleagues should never be "I told him so" or "It serves her right" or "That'll teach them," and they should never take pleasure in the misfortunes of others. The response of the principled leader will be charitable and based on a belief that the person who made the mistake will now be a much wiser person and will have learned much as a result of their experience. Wherever possible, the former colleague should be welcomed back joyfully into the company fold.[42]

7. FORGIVES OTHERS

During my managerial and academic career, I have read hundreds of books aimed at the business community, and until recently I do not think I have ever read a chapter, possibly not even a paragraph, based on the premise that leaders should exercise forgiveness within the world of work.[b] Therefore, I may be one of the first to state boldly: forgiveness should be part of the principled leader's daily practice as he or she interacts with others, including during times and conditions that are potentially hostile.

---

b. As I point out in other parts of this book, there are signs that this position is changing, and some newer books speak of the function and benefit of forgiveness.

"What?" I can hear some reader shout, "Have you lived an isolated life? Don't you know what it's like out there? It's a jungle." That is true; it is a jungle in too many places, and I assure you that I have lived "out there" and experienced some pretty hostile environments. I have not lived a sheltered life; I know what life on the "shop-floor" can be like, and despite all of that I am confident in my assertion that forgiveness should be a part of everyone's daily life in the office, factory, or wherever you happen to work. Let me explain why I take this view.

First, it is because forgiving those who ask to be forgiven is the right thing to do, and if anyone doubts the veracity of that statement then I suggest they read the literature on the practice of forgiveness. I know many people live in a world where those raised on liberal attitudes are reluctant to lay down any hard and fast general principle, but I believe that forgiveness of those who ask to be forgiven is a universal truth, and I also believe that such widespread practice would transform relationships in work and across wider society.

Second, failing to exercise forgiveness as a general principle is likely to create bitterness and resentment in an individual that will gnaw away at their spirit and make them less of a man or a woman. These two quotations have challenged me more times than I am willing to admit:

> We forgive not merely to fulfil some higher law of morality; we do it for ourselves. The first and often the only person to be healed by forgiveness is the person who does the forgiveness....when we genuinely forgive we set a prisoner free and then discover that the prisoner was us.
>
> —Philip Yancy[43]

> And because we are forgiven people we will be able to summon the motivation and the power to forgive. As we determine not to hold the grievance against our brother ... gradually the heart catches up with the head and forgiveness, repeatedly reiterated, becomes part of us and enters deep into the wounded feelings.
>
> —Michael Green[44]

"That's hard," someone says. Of course it is hard; who suggested it might be easy? But there is another dimension that is even harder: what attitude should be shown towards those who have not asked for forgiveness, those people who actually take pleasure in being a "tough cookie," who enjoy riding roughshod over people more junior to them in the organisation? If I were writing a book on forgiveness I would take a diversion at this point and write a thousand words or so on whether a person should forgive those who have not requested forgiveness—but in this book I will limit myself to some practical examples.

I realise how difficult it can be when someone has treated another unfairly, has made scathing and untrue remarks behind their back, has decided to attack them without reason, and other similar behaviour. In these circumstances, there are three choices in my opinion: a person can fight back, making use of the various resources at their disposal (and there are extreme circumstances when it is right and proper to engage the services of a lawyer or someone else); or they can take it lying down and allow themselves to be treated like a doormat, allowing people to walk over them and treat them like a wimp (which I would not recommend); or they can decide to take the moral high ground in their response: they can decide to act reasonably and graciously.

The principled leader understands that in dealing with one of life's "tough cookies," their adversary is expert in fighting fierce battles and actually enjoys, and obtains energy from, the heat of combat. There is nothing they like better than a good and dirty fight; they are prepared for the battle; they have attack and defence tactics available and "on-call." In some ways they are daring the principled leader to test them, to see how strong they are, to show that someone as puny as a principled leader (yuck!) cannot overcome them! What they are not expert at handling is grace and reason, and they often have little idea how to react—graciousness and reason can become a Trojan horse to take them by surprise.

As I said earlier, I do not live outside the real world, isolated from the realities of everyday life, and I know that even gracious and reasonable people can be sacked unfairly or treated badly in their working lives. However, I also know this: to react with grace and reason when being badly treated represents a victory for the principled leader, and if there is a need to leave that particular employment then there is far more chance of being employed elsewhere. Others will recognise a leader of principle and perceive a "big" person, someone who refuses to stoop to the lower levels of others.[45]

8. DEMONSTRATES FAIRNESS

In companies where salary is linked to individual performance and a range of personal factors, it is easier to appreciate a reward system where wide fluctuations exist based on the owner's preferences and the performance of the individual. For those who work in large organisations, where there may be a bureaucratic method of salary determination based on job-related criteria rather than on the person holding the post, it is almost inconceivable to envisage a payment system established solely on the predilections of the owner of the company.

Whatever the system and whatever the degree of objectivity or subjectivity in salary determination, there is a general principle at stake for the principled leader: it concerns being generally content with one's lot. There may be legitimate concerns about the niceties of the remuneration strategies or aspects of wage comparability, but the general rule still holds true. Applying this principle does not mean that an individual should not have goals and aspirations or that they merely resign themselves to accepting the "hand" that life has dealt them. That smacks of fatalism, if not defeatism, and certainly lacks any sense of wishing to improve oneself. Nor does it mean that the principled leader should not set about to right real wrongs, but the general rule does mean that one's goal should be contentment and that circumstances should never be allowed to turn the principled leader into the type of person who is constantly dissatisfied with what they have achieved and the opportunities they have been given.

Dissatisfied people are a real drain: they complain about most of the things they experience; they may well be envious of other people and have to cope with feelings of jealousy; and they find it impossible to see any glass as being half full—for them the glass is always half empty. It is one of life's joys to be with people who are satisfied and set out to live life to the full. They are able to count their blessings, to appreciate what they have, to realise that their wealth is substantially more than that of the vast percentage of humankind, and as a result they "cut their coat according to the cloth" and find that most of life's (reasonable) pleasures are within their reach.

This does not mean that the principled leader should not attempt to improve their education, career, income, and whatever else inspires or drives them, but it does mean that as they attempt to improve their position they should have an attitude that is content with what they have already achieved: instead of being envious, they should decide to enjoy the good things in life that are already within their grasp. Being in a constant state of dissatisfaction leads to a miserable life, and people who are satisfied with their lot lead far more pleasant lives.[46]

9. ACTS RELIABLY

Dependable, reliable, committed, and trustworthy: just some of the words that come to mind when considering the ideal type of employee and, in turn, the ideal type of principled leader one should aim to become.

A company will often spell out in detail the attributes or characteristics it requires in its employees. The company may also detail the values by which business is to be conducted and assert the importance of living by those values, and rightly so. However, it is impossible to legislate for the conduct of individuals within the company, and it is such a bonus to have employees whose personal code contains a commitment to dependability, reliability, commitment, trust, and much more. It is far easier to build a set of corporate values and employee attributes upon such a basic code of behaviour.

If the comments in the last paragraph are difficult to accept, then consider someone who has tried to build a company with people who cannot be depended on, who are unreliable, who lack commitment, and who have to be supervised continually. Sometimes it is not wholly the fault of the people; perhaps they have been led badly by a previous management team or have experienced conditions that made them wary and even cynical. However, in most circumstances no one should resort to blaming past leaders for a lack of basic standards in their work, as there is always need for conduct to be based on values that include reliability, commitment, and trust, and for those standards to be followed sincerely.[47]

10. ENCOURAGES GROWTH

When my youngest son, Simon, was about six years old we took him to the fair visiting our town, and to his delight he won a goldfish. He was thrilled, and we took the goldfish home and found a suitable temporary glass jar for our new pet. Within a short time the goldfish, which by this time had acquired the name Sam, grew and we needed to buy him a proper goldfish bowl. Sam continued to grow, and in a matter of a few months it was clear that Sam needed a larger bowl, and we were given a small aquarium by one of our neighbours. Sam loved his new aquarium and spent his time happily improving his breaststroke and backstroke—or, at least, the piscine equivalent.

As time went on, Simon began to lose interest in Sam, and Sam continued to grow. In fact we became concerned that even his new aquarium was no longer large enough for him so, with Simon's full agreement, it was decided that the best thing for Sam was for him to be given to another neighbour who had a garden pond with many fish. Sam moved from aquarium to pond and Simon would visit him each week. One day Simon reported to us two amazing facts: first, Sam had continued to grow and was now the size of a small trout (you may have to allow some room for exaggeration here) and, second, Sam had become the proud mother of a number of small goldfish. Immediately, Sam became Samantha!

I have told this story at many conferences under the heading *personal growth*, to delegates from numerous countries of the world, and all of them spot the tale's central message immediately and charitably accept the difficulty of allocating a gender to a small goldfish. The message is, if people are placed in the right environment and given proper support, then they are likely to grow—not physically, but they grow in terms of the contribution they can make to the company. I have seen this principle take effect in all sorts of organizations; when given the right training, the right development opportunity, and a supportive learning environment, people inevitably grow and make a major contribution to their companies.

Naturally, this principle does not apply to each and every individual, but it does apply to the majority of people as long as the conditions are conducive to such growth. Overseeing the application of this principle is one of the principled leader's major challenges and also one of the most rewarding. It is such a joy to see individuals grow, develop to their full potential, and make an even greater contribution than anyone had thought possible.[48]

11. VALUES PEOPLE

Allow me to tell a story about two people I once worked with: one was Mr. Goodman and one was Mr. Badman.[c]

Mr. Goodman was a senior person in the company, but he made sure that his position never prevented him from speaking with the other employees of the organisation, irrespective of their status in life. Whether the employee was the office junior or a senior manager, a catering assistant or the head of sales, Mr. Goodman would always have time for a quick chat and made a point of treating everyone with the same courtesy. He liked people; he respected them and valued the contribution they all made to the success of the enterprise. And the people liked Mr. Goodman. His career went from strength to strength, and as he prospered he still found time to treat everyone as a special employee and to take notice of what they did for the business.

Mr. Badman could charm the birds out the trees if he wanted. He was eloquent and able to talk about most work-related subjects in an impressive manner. He knew that for him to be even more successful he needed to have a talented group of people reporting to him who were aligned with his key objectives. Over a short period of time he assembled an impressive team of people, and he spoke well of them because he knew that they could enhance his reputation within the company and the wider community. But as time went on, first one member of Mr. Badman's team, and then another, became dispensable—they no longer served a useful purpose in terms of

---

c. I trust that I will be excused some gender stereotyping for the sake of this one story.

enhancing Mr. Badman's reputation—and so he dumped them. There was no great argument between them; Mr. Badman just stopped inviting them to key events, and when they were in meetings together he chose to ignore them. Slowly they got the message and felt that they had been used and then discarded; Mr. Badman had only shown an interest in them to enhance his own career objectives. Mr. Badman's career continued to expand until one day his boss dumped him—he left the company and was not missed by many.

The story of Messrs. Goodman and Badman is a true story based on real characters, although the account has been somewhat embellished. These characters exist in all organisations, and the Mr. Goodmen (and Mrs. Goodwomen) need to be lauded and the Mr. Badmen (and Mrs. Badwomen) need to be seen for what they are— merely people who use other people for their own ends. The principled leader meets the needs of other people and respects them, without discrimination and without some assessment of their position in the hierarchy and their utility to enhance the leader's career. [49]

12. CHOOSES PROPER PRIORITIES

This is rather a sombre point and concerns issues being faced by many people these days: it is the matter of having wrong priorities.

Irrespective of personal circumstances, principled leaders will check regularly that their priorities stand up to scrutiny, that essentials have been placed first, and that they do not make idols out of the inconsequential things in life. Some leaders worship their profession and see it as the be all and end all of their existence; others worship the pursuit of wealth or fame; and for others it will be some other enticement that becomes their idol. Principled leaders understand clearly that their priorities need to be legitimate ones, and they see to it that they live their lives according to worthwhile priorities, adhering to those that will stand the test of time. They are priorities to be proud of when they retire and when they arrive at their last day on earth—I did warn this was a sombre point.

For those who have difficulties in this area they need to be humble and speak to someone about it, although they may be at a stage where they do not yet recognise that there are problems to be addressed. The worst thing that can be done is to adopt a position that attacks the very solution to one's needs, a response that is often born out of arrogance and the assumption that one already has the answer to all needs. These are important things to consider and centrally important to the principled leader.[50]

13. SHOWS CONSIDERATION AND DETERMINATION

The principled leader is open to reasoned argument and prepared to listen to a persuasive and objective case, but is not the type of leader whose mind can be changed by someone who just continues to repeat their argument, believing that the drip, drip, drip effect of reiterating the same old and tired points of debate will finally wear down the leader's resolve. The principled leader will listen intently to all the points someone has to make and will be prepared to change their mind when circumstances change or new information demands it, but when this occurs the principled leader makes sure that people do not believe that a repetition of the same old debating points has made the leader reverse previous decisions.[51]

14. KNOWS WHEN TO ACT

Principled leaders are capable of observing analytically those things taking place around them and learn from those observations. They appreciate that the very essence of learning is to take the knowledge they have acquired and to translate that information into new and improved actions.

Also, the principled leader understands that timeliness is an essential facet of action: a time when it is best for certain things to happen and a time when it is best not for them to happen. Some people know this timing intuitively—an intuition honed after many years of experience: they know when to take action and they know when to delay action; they are able to read the runes and exercise sound judgement. Such people are extremely valuable, especially when there is need to judge whether or not to launch a new initiative or to engage in some aspect of change management. The young and inexperienced principled leader learns from such people, as this sense of timeliness is an invaluable capability for any young leader to acquire. Many sound initiatives have been lost because they were launched at injudicious times, and some initiatives that deserved being lost were made to work purely because of timing. The principled leader knows that the best of all outcomes usually occurs when a sound initiative is launched at the most appropriate time.[52]

15. BECOMES A SERVANT

Earlier in the book I encouraged those who were unfamiliar with the concept of servant leadership to access Web sites and books to obtain a basic understanding of this leadership philosophy.[53] I encourage you to look at the literature and find out more about this important concept.

Becoming a servant-leader is a challenge that combines many contrasting and apparently contradicting characteristics: servanthood and leadership; power and humility; authority and submission; and much else. The principled leader knows that there is a choice to be made, namely, is the leader willing to become a servant who leads, not a leader who serves, a true servant-leader?

It is relatively easy for leaders to become puffed up with pride, through overemphasising their undoubted achievements, and although this is understandable, especially in those who are young and inexperienced, it really is quite distasteful and results in people talking about the proud leader behind his or her back. It is far better for the principled leader to become a humble servant who leads.[54] In fact, the challenge is great, but the rewards for all concerned are substantial.

16. MANAGES CHANGE

New ideas, new ways of doing things, new ways of looking at a problem—to many people the very word *new* is anathema and can guarantee their opposition to the idea. "I don't care what it is, if it's new and I've got to change my ways then I'm against it," is their response. A person may not actually utter these words, but the phrase represents the individual's deep-rooted reaction to change, and it is that built-in opposition, or to state it positively that built-in preference for the status quo, that makes bringing about change or introducing new ideas so difficult for the leader.

People become attached to things as they are; they do not want to experience change. But, the principled leader realises that there are times when (to use a metaphor) placing a patch over something that is torn becomes foolish. Everyone should know that when the patch is tested, as undoubtedly it will be, it will tear, and there will be a need for further extensive remedial work. Similarly, new ideas can only be put into minds that are sufficiently flexible to handle them, that are capable of considering them robustly, and are able to allow them to ferment without causing undue pressure on the mind, the vessel that is holding them.[55]

Summary—The Principled Leader:

1. Establishes solid foundations.
2. Knows their people.
3. Finds the right levers.
4. Creates friendships.
5. Utilises talents.
6. Practises stewardship.
7. Forgives others.
8. Demonstrates fairness.
9. Acts reliably.
10. Encourages growth.
11. Values people.
12. Chooses proper priorities.
13. Shows consideration and determination.
14. Knows when to act.
15. Becomes a servant.
16. Manages change.

CHAPTER 6
The Resolute Leader

∙∙∙

This chapter has been written, and inserted at this juncture in the book, for those people who have reached a point in their career where they have told themselves, or perhaps exclaimed to others: "That's it! I've had it—no more, I'm giving up!" and find it difficult to cope with my exhortations to be purposeful and principled and exemplary (as the next chapter will encourage). You feel you have given your best, tried your hardest, but whatever you were concerned with seems to have ended in failure. Or you may feel that other people in whom you placed faith have let you down: they didn't do what they said they would do and without their crucial contribution your attempts failed. Or, it may be that you bit off more than you could chew; you feel overstretched and exhausted and have reached the end of the road. Whatever the reason, you have had enough, and there is no more energy left in the tank, your enthusiasm has gone, your confidence has taken a bad knock. and the only sensible thing to do as far as you can see is to give in, call it a day, learn from the experience (hopefully), and move on with your life. It is time to leave this to other people, to see if they can make a success where you experienced failure.

If that describes you, then I want to assure you that I do understand; I really do. I am also aware that if you have read the previous two chapters, then your reaction may have been dismissive. You may have thought: "If only you knew what I've been through then you'd realise I don't want to be purposeful and principled. I tried and it all went horribly wrong!" I do understand, honestly, and that is why the alternative title for this chapter could be, "Never Say '*Never Again*'— Usually There Is a Way Through." I know you may have had some difficult experiences, ones that caused you distress and, therefore, before I encourage you to be an exemplary leader, I want to show you, through four very different experiences, that there is a way back for most people, whatever you have been through.

Some readers may be wondering what on earth the opening of this chapter is getting at: this is not a description of you at all. You relish the opportunity to take on a challenge, to make things happen in your company; you are someone who has not encountered much opposition or any sense of failure in your career. If this describes you, then let me suggest that you count your many blessings (or lucky stars if you prefer), because you have lived a charmed life. If you are such a fortunate person, then may I further suggest that you read this chapter slowly, paying particular attention to what it has to say, because there might (and probably will) come a day when you set out to make substantial changes to improve practices and performance in your company and encounter strong opposition, only to be seen to have failed in the eyes of your colleagues. That experience is fairly common, and the good news is that if you react properly to the experience it can be the making of you.

To write such comments is not being unduly negative, merely a recognition of the reality of life for the vast majority of leaders. Many initiatives fail, and leaders who are constructive and positive and want to transform the way in which things are done often face unfair and undeserved criticism and misrepresentation. Unless the leaders are strong, which they usually are, then they will be faced with the real temptation to give it all up and become merely a yes-man or a yes-woman, reluctantly accepting the status quo in everything they encounter, never trying to rock the boat to see if there are better ways of getting things done in their place of work, and as a result they become dispirited.

Why have these paragraphs been written in such a dramatic and negative manner? Why do they remind you of the real possibility of failure instead of encouraging you to think that you can transform the world if only you think about this book and apply some of its principles? The answer to that question is easy: it is because life just isn't that simple. If you are the type of person who wants to see a transformed work environment, then it is likely that you have tried many times to make significant differences in your company. You have led change initiatives, and it is likely that you have experienced both success and failure: that you have many accolades to exhibit, but also scars and emotional hurts to show for your efforts.

Be assured that what follows will be an encouragement to everyone: to those who have experienced success and failure and usually a combination of both. But the chapter does not encourage a form of leadership triumphalism, as if everything in the garden is always rosy; this chapter, and the whole book, is based on a realism that has been forged in the school of hard knocks and, thankfully, the school of many deserved and undeserved blessings. This chapter takes a hard look at adversity in its various forms and shows how it can become a source of strength in your life. In the section headed "Four Stories of Hope" four apparent worst-case scenarios are discussed and used as a potential springboard to encourage everyone to believe they can make a difference. It may be a small difference, but never doubt the overall effect of tens of thousands of such contributions: they can help change the world.

Four Stories of Hope

These four stories are different in terms of when they occurred and why they happened, and one of the stories seems to concern trees instead of human beings. Each of the first three stories concerns someone who had an unexpected and unwelcome event in their life. In the first story, the event was self-inflicted, a consequence of a loss of personal courage. In the second story, the unwelcome event was a result of an accident. In the third story, it was a consequence of a decision made by another party altogether. The fourth story is taken from the natural world and perfectly illustrates a principle concerning life in general. Each of the stories concerns triumph in the face of apparent temporary or even permanent defeat, and each of the stories has been included to encourage you to take hold of what life may have thrown at you, to encourage you to believe that you should never say "never again."

STORY 1: SIMON PETER

The first example is taken from an event that took place a long time ago, but it is such a dramatic event, and one that resonates so effectively with experiences today, that I decided to include it. If you think such an old story cannot be relevant to you, please jump to the next two examples, taken from contemporary life, although I warn you that the fourth story will encourage you to think laterally, to say the least.

This is the story of Simon Peter, one of Christ's twelve disciples, and describes how he let his leader down after vowing to stand by him no matter what might have to be endured for this loyalty. The account, taken from St. Luke's[56] narrative, starts with Jesus telling Peter, "I have prayed for you that your own faith may not fail." Peter appears to be horrified at the thought that he would fail Jesus in some way and tells Jesus that he is ready to serve him in prison, even to die for him. And he means it. Peter seems to understand that following Jesus will involve his disciples in some form of suffering, yet he is confident that he will be able to face up to whatever comes his way. Peter declares boldly, "Lord, I am ready to go with you to prison and to death!" But Jesus knew Peter better than Peter knew himself and predicts that "the cock will not crow this day" until Peter would deny him three times. Once would be bad enough, twice would be dreadful, but Peter would do it three times.

Eventually, Jesus is arrested and taken to the house of the high priest, and Peter is described as following at a distance. A servant girl sees him and says, "This man also was with him," and Peter denies it. Then someone else sees Peter and says, "You also are one of them," and Peter replies, "Man, I am not!" About an hour later someone else says, "Surely this man also was with him," and Peter contends, "Man, I do not know what you are talking about!" and as Peter uttered those words the cock crowed. St. Luke says that "The Lord turned and looked at Peter," and Peter, realising what he had done, went outside and "wept bitterly." Peter must have felt terrible. He might well have thought, "I've let him down. He trusted me and I failed him. I can't go on. I'm going to pack it in."

These are dramatic events that raise an important question in the context of this chapter. How do you deal with a sense of failure in your life? I say a sense of failure because often you have not failed; it is just that you feel you have failed, and that feeling is just as bad as real failure. Unless you are a very special person, the sort of person who has never failed someone, you will know those times in your life when you feel that you have disappointed someone in your family or at work—they were expecting you to act in a particular way and you did not. You felt that you failed, let yourself and others down: "I failed! I said I was going to do it and I didn't do it." You felt a real sense of failure, for whatever reason, and it was a pretty bad feeling that you can still feel today.

If experiencing real failure and a sense of failure are things everyone has to cope with in their lives, from time to time and to differing degrees, then the experience of Peter has something important to teach people in the twenty-first century. There are two parts of the conversation between Jesus and Peter that provide helpful insights.

First, Jesus tells Peter that he has prayed for him. The prayer is not that the immediate battle and failure will be prevented, as failure seems to be an inevitable part of life; Jesus' request is that Peter's "faith may not fail," that there won't be any permanent damage to Peter's faith as a result of his failure. Jesus knows that in a matter of hours Peter will deny him three times, and yet Jesus, as Peter's leader, is stepping in to ensure that Peter will not make a total renunciation of his faith as a result of these failures.

Second, although Peter will experience failure, he will become a wiser and stronger person as a result of the experience and then will be able to strengthen his fellow disciples. He will have learned that failure is possible, that the flesh is weak, and as a result Peter will be able to strengthen other people. It is as if Jesus is saying to Peter, "You will deny me and you will weep bitter tears, but the result will be that you will be better able to help your brothers who are going through their challenges." Peter will be able to strengthen his companions because he will understand how easy it is to fail, and he will be able to show them, from firsthand experience, that there is always an opportunity for restoration. You may have had a similar experience: if you have experienced failure it gives you more empathy and understanding to help others. It seems that even though failure is regrettable, sometimes the very best lessons you learn come as you reflect on those very failures.

What Peter did everyone is capable of doing, and so it is quite easy to empathise with Peter. When Peter saw what happened to Jesus in the next few days, he must have been heartbroken. Probably Peter could have coped better if Jesus had been angry with him or thrown him out of the group of disciples, but Peter knew that Jesus understood and that he had forgiven him. And when Peter stopped to think about it, he would begin to understand that Jesus had plans to use him in some way or other to strengthen the other disciples as a result of his own experience.

Just think what Peter had to do. There was only one way to strengthen the disciples, and that was to share with them how he had failed the Lord and what he had learned from that experience. In my vivid imagination, perhaps my overvivid imagination, I can see the disciples' weekly team briefing bulletin:

ON TUESDAY EVENING, AT 7 PM, PETER WILL SHARE WITH US HOW HE FAILED OUR LEADER THREE TIMES IN ONE DAY!!!

That takes courage and humility, and it also takes understanding friends and colleagues who are willing to learn from the experiences of others. I would like you to take part in an exercise of the imagination. This is the exercise: Peter is feeling distraught after letting down his Lord three times in the space of a few hours. Somehow, you've been transported back in time, and there you are standing in front of Peter, and he asks you for advice. What would you say to him to comfort him in his hour of need? I guess that first of all you would empathise with him; then you would want to show him that you really did understand how he felt. Then you might say to him: "No matter how you feel Peter, you can be restored; you will recover from the experience you've just gone through. You really have to try and trust that good can come even out of bad." You might also say: "Do you remember what Jesus said to you? He said that as a result of this failure you would be able to strengthen the other disciples. I know you're feeling bad about it right now, but you will learn from this experience, and it will be of help to you and to many other people." You might finish speaking to Peter by saying: "Peter, this will take time, perhaps a long time, and you may always regret what happened, but you know that your life will help many people."

And, what is true for Peter can most certainly become true for you.

STORY 2: CHRISTINE[a]

The first time I met Christine she was twenty-one years old, recently graduated (in economics, if I remember rightly) and even more recently appointed into the department I had been asked to lead. Within a short period of time I spotted her managerial potential, and over the next two years she undertook valuable project work. With my encouragement, she then left the department to take up an appointment, at corporate level within the same organisation, which would see her career develop rapidly over the next decade. She was highly regarded in her chosen managerial field. When an opportunity arose for her to rejoin me in a new venture I had been asked to lead, I jumped at the chance to recruit her and looked forward to the contribution I knew she would make. Life did not turn out quite as expected.

Her story is told in her own words:

There I was, aged thirty-four, just divorced, and pursuing a lifelong dream to do a parachute jump. Well, all did not go according to plan— time for a rethink and reframe! I ended up hitting the ground too hard and sustained a broken back with an incomplete spinal cord injury.

Until then my work had been as an organisation development consultant in the National Health Service, specializing in change and leadership development.

The accident happened in 2000—the millennium year and the second year of Wales' devolved constitutional powers—and as I was completely immobile for three months there was a lot of opportunity for reflection in all sorts of ways: on me, on my purpose in life, on my emerg-

a. Christine Davies wrote most of this section and I am very grateful to her.

ing country, and on our world—a paralyzed individual or a paralyzed world, or both?

I moved through the stages of rehabilitation. This was the most difficult, painful, and challenging time. I felt angry, impotent, complete terror and fear, and at times, utter despair. There was a loss of personal identity, femininity, and even personhood and worth. I realized that all I could do was one hour and one day at a time—"baby steps." Then over time I realized that these baby steps were adding up, and all of a sudden—I could get out of bed—I could transfer to a wheelchair—I could even learn to use one. As I started to go home for weekends and be surrounded by the love and support of my family and friends, I realized that I might be able to start to build a new life too.

No one could experience an event like that and not be changed— I chose consciously that I had lessons to learn, and these are just some that have emerged so far.

1. Where There Is a Will There's a Way

Creative solutions can always be found if the will and positive intent are there. How many times have I had access challenges that seemed insurmountable? I may have had to get on my hands and knees, crawl, or whatever it took to get where I needed to go. Yet, I do hate being excluded when there is absolutely no reason for it—then I get angry! My biggest challenge is being able to trust and recognize my interdependence with others—for someone of my independence that has been hard.

2. Nothing Is Impossible

If you really believe and want something enough, you can make it happen. In my experience, it has involved bashing through the doors sometimes or seeking different ways of opening the doors, for example, automation, or by simply relying on others to help me achieve my goal by holding the door open.

If I believed what they told me about what's possible and if I'd thought about all of the obstacles, I wouldn't get out of bed any morning. My experience tells me that attitude and positive belief are everything. You just have to trust that you have the resources within and around you to overcome the challenges or, to express it differently, the opportunities as they present themselves.

3. Hope, Faith, and Belief

It can be easy to get into a spiral of despair. Hope has such an important role in providing that light in the dark. Faith and belief are all part of a bigger picture, and systemic learning of life lessons for growth has really helped me. So rather than sinking into a pit of despair and believing that I was being punished or persecuted (though I have lived there somewhat), I have chosen something else.

Now, eight years later, I can appreciate what a profound, prolific, and powerful phase for learning it has been in my life.

4. Fun / Play / Laughter

A sense of humour and fun can so dissolve tension sometimes and enable us to cope and, when we play about, to find creative solutions that we never expected. Also, with this type of deep learning—be it individual or systemic—it can be pretty tough stuff. So the ability to take ourselves lightly, to explore, to play around a little, to make mistakes and to laugh at them is a crucial creative release.

Trusting yourself and those around you also becomes crucial, knowing that someone cares, that someone will be there to hold you if you fall and that you will all support each other—make you braver than you would be while acting alone.

It's what makes the little baby steps have the potential to become giant leaps and release transformational powers.

5. Follow the Energy of "Yes"

Like me, you've probably met loads of "naysayers" and "doomers." We all know when we have been subject to a "psychic vampire" or "energy stealing" attack; we feel drained and we remain stuck. The same is true for organizations.

Well, back to conscious choice again—I have become discerning and choosy about how I expend my energy and on what.

Last year, while at a servant leadership conference in South Africa, I heard Margaret Wheatley talk about "whale energy." She put up a slide of a humpback whale in the middle of the air, completely out of the water, and said, "This whale thinks it can fly—so it does!" What a lesson to us all: FOLLOW THE ENERGY OF YES!

I recently went back to South Africa, and I was able to witness examples of amazing courage and commitment to transformation and social change in the townships. This was being achieved by people who were truly inspirational and working locally to better the communities in which they lived—especially for the future of the next generation. They had made a conscious choice to take those baby steps to make that difference, and it was happening.

I am now an organisation development consultant and coach and a social entrepreneur, aiming to release the individual and collective creative potential, which is the key purpose of leadership as I see it.

In this powerful and moving personal account, we can see how a set of experiences led to a substantial transformation in Christine's outlook on life. For others the experiences and changes need not be so dramatic or fundamental, but Christine's story is a moving example of how it is possible to overcome adversity and learn from even the most trying of circumstances.

STORY 3: MICHAEL[b]

Michael's story is about being let down by other people and how that experience, which was difficult to confront at the time, did not result in lasting disappointment and discouragement but led to the discovery of opportunities that would otherwise never have arisen.

Michael had been employed by a well-known horticultural company in the east of England for four years. His success in his job had led to a promotion into the marketing department twelve months earlier and, in two months' time, he was about to be married. Then the bombshell arrived: the company was experiencing difficult conditions, wanted to reduce its cost base, and Michael's post was one of many to be declared "redundant." His employment would

---

b. I interviewed Michael Wheatley to write this section and he approved the final draft. My thanks go to him.

come to an end with the company a matter of days before his wedding. Not the most auspicious of starts to his new life.

Instead of feeling despondent, he saw it as a new opportunity, as he had found the marketing role to be unsatisfying but would never have resigned the post with his marriage just ahead. Being made redundant was in many ways a relief, as it enabled him to do what he and his bride-to-be wanted to do: they, now married, sold the house, packed their possessions into a newly acquired van, and set off on an adventure that took them to the Isle of Skye, in the north of Scotland. There, they bought a cottage, endured initial unemployment and a severely cold winter, but over time set up a small business specialising in building, woodwork, and architectural services. The physical trial of establishing themselves in this new and strange environment "made our marriage, as we were both in it together."

That may seem like an unusual move on their part, but it was the right move for them. They saw it as an adventure: Michael's wife was young and "game for action," and Michael, still in his early thirties, had a strong self-belief that "…if you want to do it, then do it. You can do it if you really decide you want to do it. Within reason, if you want to do it you can do it."

I was intrigued by this attitude to life, and Michael assured me that this was not a family trait inherited from his parents or present in other members of his family. However, what is most revealing is that Michael had known earlier tragedy in his life. Sometime before, his first wife had died following a long illness, and this made him believe that no one knows how long they will be on this earth; so it was unreasonable to think that you could do something forever or, conversely in his case, that "if you don't do it now it may be too late." It seemed that on the basis of what he had been through, he could better deal with uncertainties, set new priorities, deal positively with minor disappointments (such as losing a job), and welcome new starts, genuinely seeing them as opportunities rather than calamities.

After nearly seven years on the Isle of Skye, they moved their home, rather speculatively once more, to a rural community in west Wales. As he waited for planning permission to build their own home, he worked on a farm, then spent twelve years working for a management training company that disappointingly ended once more in redundancy with the closure of the business. He then developed his own company, one that met the needs of clients, supplied him sufficient income, and worked in a way that suited Michael's personality and skills. In his new environment he also refound his long discarded faith, becoming, over a period of time, an indispensable part of the local church community and, at the time of writing, has been accepted for a training programme that will lead to his becoming a priest within the Anglican Church.

An unusual set of experiences, in many ways, and I asked him what he had learned on his journey. Michael gave me what he called his "general lessons" that he would commend to other people: First, you have to believe that every cloud does have a silver lining and that good can come out of what appears to be distinctly not good when it happens to you. Second, you have to be prepared to do almost anything to provide "bread" for your family, and as you work hard at something, perhaps not the ideal job at that point in time, then other opportunities will present themselves, but usually only to those who have an optimistic outlook on life. Third, as an individual you have to be adaptable and creative in finding solutions. You must be proactive rather than reactive. That has to be the way to deal with the circumstances that life has the habit of throwing at you. Fourth, Michael came to realise that there was a spiritual dimension to what had taken place, and was taking place, in his life. When we spoke he could look back over almost thirty years and he could now see it as one whole journey. Prior to meeting his first wife, he had turned his back on God. When she became ill he had gone through periods of questioning and experienced feelings of guilt at his own happiness. Then when he rediscovered his faith, so many of life's challenges fell into place—in a strange way, they began to make some sort of sense. He felt as if each stage of his life had been led, in some way or other, and what he had gone through had been a progressive journey, even though he had not realised that he was on a journey at all. No one understands pain and suffering, and certainly there is no attempt in this account to minimise or rationalise those events. On a lesser scale, why some people lose their jobs and others do not is also often difficult to explain, and what his story encourages people to believe is that good can come out of the most discouraging of circumstances and that having a positive outlook—in other words, never saying "never again"—is to be commended.

STORY 4: THE DEADWOOD TREE SPECIALIST

The fourth and final example is taken from the world of nature. A regular walk of mine takes me through the National Trust Park near my home, and on one of these walks I stopped to admire the way in which the buds of a horse chestnut tree were bursting into life. A matter of weeks before it had looked as if the tree might be dead; the leaves had gone, the branches were bare, and yet here it was showing every sign of being full of life. I stood in wonder at the cycle of this tree: from its seemingly dead state, to its leaves and sticky buds, and then the fruit that would attract children as they started to collect the conkers. I had only been there a minute or so when someone shouted: "Do you like trees?" I was taken aback but murmured something in response, and a young man came over and announced that he was an expert on trees; he was a deadwood specialist. My facial response asked, "A what?" He explained his role and even gave me some notes explaining to conservationists his important role in life. Unfortunately, I misplaced those notes, but it was easy to discover from the Internet that managing deadwood is an important component of forest maintenance, and an extremely interesting metaphor.

Consider this October 2004 extract from the World Wildlife Fund's report

Deadwood: Living Forests
Up to a third of European forest species depend on veteran trees and deadwood for their survival. Deadwood is providing habitat, shelter, and food source for birds, bats and other mammals and is particularly important for the less visible majority of forest dwelling-species....

The WWF Web site develops this theme and adds:

Forests with dead and veteran trees are often much healthier and resistant to disease, pests, and climate change than young tidy forests. Deadwood keeps forests productive by

> providing organic matter and nutrients for trees, preventing
> soil erosion, and providing long-term storage for carbon....

I need hardly say that my interest in deadwood as a concept was more than a passing interest in environmental or arboricultural matters. When I read the following Chris Skellern quote on the "net" I almost chuckled:

> Branches can die for a number of reasons. Many die as a nat-
> ural process of becoming shaded out by other, higher, more
> efficient branches....Many branches die due to root damage;
> this is a common problem on development sites....Or, the
> tree may be experiencing attack from a disease....[57]

There are times in forest maintenance when action has to be taken over deadwood, but I was no longer interested in the physical aspect; my mind had already seen the potential of using deadwood as a wonderful metaphor for managerial life in the company.

How many times have I heard of a newly appointed testos-terone-charged young manager say that there is a need to clear out the *deadwood* from the organisation they have taken over? It seems the right thing to do: get rid of the old stuff, chop off what is no longer delivering results, give the younger people room to develop and an opportunity to see what they can deliver, and such like. It seems eminently sensible to them, and off they go, reducing the aver-age age of the employees through a programme of voluntary early retirement—making room for a younger, more vibrant, perform-ance-driven culture. This is one of the reasons why the average age of conference delegates is typically young to middle-aged and the num-ber of those with grey hair is relatively small, even at a time when the average age of the population is becoming older: when grey power is becoming a social phenomenon.

Do these young, up-and-coming dynamos not realise that their action in stripping bare the company of what they consider to be dead-wood will harm their future profitability rather than enhance it? Do they not see that taking out numerous people who possess years of valuable experience and knowledge of the company—organisational memory or organisational intelligence as many gurus call it—will have a deleterious effect? Are they so shortsighted as to believe that only those who can work out vigorously each morning and probably run half-marathons are worth engaging in their brave new world? And yet, that is exactly what they do: they strip out the old (which is defined as anyone over the age of fifty in some companies), classifying them as deadwood, and replace them with energetic youngsters without any real sense of the immense amount of talent based on experience, knowledge, and sound judgement that has been lost to the business. Energetic youngsters should be welcomed as important new lifeblood for the company, but not at the expense of more experienced people.

These newly appointed young managers should learn from the world of ecology that deadwood is a part of the fine balance that makes up a living system, such as an organisation. Without a fine balance in the age profile of the company the business can be damaged: too old, without lifeblood coming in at one end and there is trouble ahead; or too young, where the experience has been stripped out and the company is likely to make many mistakes. The so-called deadwood can also provide "nourishment" for other species to survive on, the sort of sustenance that is based on experience and judgement. Why is it not possible to set up a mentoring system where the older, wiser, and more experienced employees pass on their wisdom to the younger members of staff and help them to grow and mature? Surely that cannot be too difficult a process to establish. Just as the ecologists wish to break up the myths surrounding deadwood in forests, so you should spend time exploding the myths that people with grey hair are a liability to the future growth of the business. Actually, the opposite is true where the experience of the alleged deadwood is marshalled and made into an asset that contributes to growth.

The arboriculturalists teach us that three of the common causes of deadwood are: the lower branches being shaded by those higher in the organisation, oops, in the tree I meant; by root damage; and by attack from disease. All three of these can be found in the typical company. If people are kept out of the communication loop, not invited to key meetings, or not sent critical documents, then is it any wonder that they begin to look a little jaded—not quite performing as they used to perform? This then becomes a self-fulfilling prophecy, where senior and younger managers become convinced that they need to take action to remove the deadwood they have identified, or where older managers are excluded from development programmes or seem to be beyond the pale when it comes to being considered as playing a part in some new exciting venture. Again, they are excluded from where the action is taking place, and senior managers are then justified, at least in their own eyes, in taking measures to rid the company of the deadwood that is hanging around. It is perfectly true that deadwood can be caused by the onset of disease, and in such instances the older person may need welfare provision that recognises the contribution made over the years, and one would expect such action to be taken as sympathetically and respectfully as possible.

I believe very much in effective and efficient organisations, and I would be one of the first to support management action where that was necessary to transform unprofitable enterprises into ones that can make profits for the good of all, but taking action against what is perceived to be a soft target—deadwood—is an unwise action, causing far more harm than good. Deadwood can serve such a useful purpose in sustaining the life of other species, and without its contribution those very forms of life would be no more. How much more can the talents of an organisation's so-called deadwood be used as a part of a regenerative process to empower the younger person while enabling the older person to see the critical role they have to play in the future of the business.

The metaphor of *deadwood* has been used so far to challenge the ill-advised practice of many senior managers in companies but, to maintain the context of this chapter, it should also be stressed that individuals who reach a certain age should not automatically consider themselves to be too old or "past it." They have so much to contribute to the vitality of the company, for more years than they believe, and in many other cultures the older person is venerated for his or her wisdom and experience and for what can be passed on to the younger generation.

Summary: The Resolute Leader

The people used as examples in this chapter faced major setbacks in their lives, but their experiences demonstrate that the severest of obstacles can be overcome when people think positively and decide that adverse circumstances are not going to get the better of them. Naturally, some people have suffered catastrophic events, such as terrible accidents or illnesses, and through no fault of their own have never been able to recover from those setbacks. However, it is also true that many people have managed to turn a seemingly impossible situation on its head.

This summary contains twelve lessons, either taken randomly from the four stories or generated from general principles raised by a story.

1. THOSE WHO BRING ABOUT CHANGE FAIL OCCASIONALLY

People destined to bring about significant change will fail occasionally—it is impossible to be successful in each and every attempt to make things different: there will be times when events conspire against the change maker or when the person might even choose the wrong strategy to bring about the anticipated change. The experience of failure does not make the resolute leader give up, even if the temptation to throw in the towel is great, and the one-off disappointment is not seen as a pattern likely to affect future attempts at change. If anything, it makes the resolute leader more experienced and more determined to make the next change effort successful. Failure is used as a spur to success.

2. EXPERIENCING A SENSE OF FAILURE IS NOT THE SAME AS HAVING FAILED

For many people, it is the feeling of failure that prevents them from going to the next stage of a project or discovering another opportunity that could make a real difference in their place of work. Many find it hard to believe that others in the company have not really noticed that what they delivered was less than perfect, but the individual possessing this sense of failure is full of self-recriminations. Therein lies the problem to overcome: they have set standards far too high, been unrealistic in their goal setting, and promised far too much. As a result, it becomes inevitable that they cannot deliver against those inflated expectations of performance and so feel a failure. Resolute leaders have learned the importance of creating far more realistic expectations in the first place, of themselves and of others.

3. IT'S RARELY ALL OVER—THERE'S USUALLY A WAY BACK

Some people feel they have hit rock bottom, they cannot sink any lower, they cannot go on, it's all over for them…or so they think. This is a common feeling, experienced by many at some time or other in their lives, and when these feelings occur there needs to be a period of time to allow people to "lick their wounds," to feel sorry for themselves, and eventually to begin to put their lives back together. The resolute leader knows it to be a cliché, but the old phrase, "When you hit the bottom there is only one direction to go: up!" has more than a grain of truth to it. Say it at the wrong time, when someone is grieving their misfortune and when things are really bad for the individual, and it will be of little help, may cause annoyance, and will sound unsympathetic. The resolute leader knows that when said at the right time it can be an effective encouragement.

4. PUT FAILURE DOWN TO EXPERIENCE AND "START ALL OVER AGAIN"

Picking myself up, dusting myself down, and starting all over again, a sentiment inspired by the lyrics and music of Jerome Kern and Dorothy Fields, is a key weapon in the armoury of the resolute leader. The literalist or pedant will find fault in the words, but the resolute leader understands the sentiment lying behind them and believes the words contain a positive attitude that ideally everyone should possess.

Failure is an experience that most people encounter, and the important issue is what they do following that ominous meeting. Do they curl themselves up, adopting a supine position forever and a day, or do they take the disappointment on the chin, get up and dust themselves off, and start all over again? Failure, at some point or other, is an inevitable part of life, and the real challenge lies in the response to that eventuality.

5. FACE UP TO CHALLENGES; IT MAKES A PERSON STRONGER AND WISER

I heard an illustration many decades ago and, these days, it is often used for those training in martial arts and for people struggling with religious practice. It is the story of the butterfly chrysalis—I'll spare the emotional, rather drawn-out parts of the tale and cut quickly to the main point of the illustration.

If a butterfly is struggling to emerge from its chrysalis and someone decides to lend it a hand, the butterfly is likely to die, as the struggle, the fight to get out of its encasement, the beating of its wings in its escape, strengthens the wings and allows the butterfly to survive in a new environment. Misguided kindness to the butterfly harms it; the struggle enables it to be stronger and survive.

The resolute leader understands that many struggles in life enable the individual to emerge from their "chrysalis" stronger and wiser. Without the struggle things would have come too easily and the person would be unable to help others by recounting their experience.

6. LEARN TO FORGIVE OTHER PEOPLE AND YOURSELF

It is astonishing the number of people who cannot forgive themselves. Many years after making a mistake, saying the wrong thing, or performing less well than they would have liked, they can remember in detail how they erred, goofed up, fell short of the required standard, and they cannot let go of that unfortunate experience. They need to forgive themselves: to acknowledge that they made a mistake, to realise that everybody makes mistakes, to put right any hurt caused by their action or inaction, and then move on, draw a line under it, and refuse to relive those moments in the dramatic Technicolor® of their memories. This is easier said than done, but it is an essential part of being a resolute leader—resolving not to dwell on the failures of the past and moving on to pastures new.

7. HAVE A POSITIVE OUTLOOK ON LIFE

Hindsight is a wonderful concept: it allows people to see that most of the things that happened to them are not irretrievable and irredeemable. The resolute leader will attempt to build a dimension of hindsight into current thought processes, to help maintain a sense of proportion—whatever minor skirmishes they encounter, things will probably work themselves out in the end. The resolute leader has learned that there is usually a means of adjusting circumstances to make them more palatable: they make plans and work hard, are not cavalier in their attitudes, and believe that future problems will not be insurmountable with measured adjustments to plans.

These resolute leaders are positive and realistic individuals and have learned to dispose of negative thoughts in the trashcan; as a result, they are more successful in the things that matter. They have experience of other incidents that worked out fairly well and have a mindset that has absorbed the precious insight from Mark Twain: "Most of the things I worried about in life never happened."[c]

8. SHARE EXPERIENCES WITH OTHERS AND LEARN FROM THEM

For many years I have wanted to run a conference called: "The Two Biggest Mistakes I Ever Made and What I Learned from Them." Imagine such a conference title. Who would enroll as delegates? Who would be willing to speak? Would the speakers be honest rather than self-righteous—the sort who would say: "The biggest mistake I ever made was to underestimate the love of the American/British people"?

---

c. I know I used a variation of this quote in chapter 4, but it is such a wise comment that I decided to use it again.

What a wonderful day would be had by one and all if the delegates entered into it with an honest desire to learn from one another.

The resolute leader is unlikely to need one of these conferences because he or she makes it happen on an individual basis by talking with someone who will understand their circumstances and by taking many positives from such reflection.

9. LOOK FOR THE OPPORTUNITIES THAT COME ALONG FROM TIME TO TIME

The resolute leader tries to see change as an opportunity rather than a threat. While not racing around the corner without due care and attention, they do know of times when what waits around the corner can become one of the best decisions or experiences in their lives. They pay due attention, aware of those who have made dramatic career changes and come unstuck and, with sensible caution, look for what might open up.

Imagine what could happen: being your own boss may be the right choice; going off in another direction perhaps; finding meaning through a different lifestyle; joining another major corporation for the career best suited to you and your family; or many other such things. Be prepared for these opportunities.

10. BRING ACTIONS INTO LINE WITH PERSONAL BELIEFS

Many feel their work environment has conditioned them, or semi-programmed them, to act in a way inconsistent with the real them—they say things they do not believe and follow through with (what feels like) involuntary actions. The resolute leader adjusts their life to speak and act in ways consistent with their beliefs, releasing the person that over time has become subdued and held captive within. They may want to express their concern for the sustainability of the environment, or become more driven in their business goals, or emphasise the social responsibilities of corporations alongside their financial imperatives, or place a greater focus on individual performance. During periods of change resolute leaders welcome the opportunity to move in a direction that enables their personal belief system to be more in harmony with their actions. This is far better than objecting to all change and resenting its impact.

11. NEVER WRITE ANYTHING OR ANYONE OFF

It is quite amazing how an experience or a person from many years before can become significant at a later point in a career. Writing someone off is wrong in principle, but it is also wrong from a tactical point of view: you never know when there may be an opportunity to work together once more, and it is a wise person who maintains those contact details and keeps communication channels open.

The resolute leader respects the experience and knowledge of others and recognises that the combined worth of expertise (that of the resolute leader and the contact) is far greater than anything to be achieved individually. The resolute leader realises the extent to which different organisational systems and structures inevitably have some form of connectivity, a sense of things being linked together in an intricate web, and it is far better to realise this principle at the start of a career, ensuring that good relationships and contacts are maintained properly and sensitively.

12. COMMIT TO MAKING THINGS BETTER

Managers in various sectors of the economy use a well-known idiom to indicate their belief that if something is working reasonably well—"If it ain't broke, don't fix it"—then it should be left alone. Some leadership writers use the popular phrase to exemplify one of the main differences between management and leadership: the manager will say, "Don't fix it," and the leader will say, "Break it," so that it can be made even better. This may be an artificial and contrived differentiation between leadership and management, but the truth within the argument is that settling for the status quo is rarely the motivation of the leader. The resolute leader (and, in truth, many managers) will want to make things better, to seek improvement, to see continuous advancement in the services and products under their responsibility. They will not settle for the status quo but, rather, accept the ultimate challenge of making things better.

Conclusion

This chapter has presented four scenarios illustrating the various trials that four different people have overcome. Their experiences can be used as a springboard to encourage others to believe that they can make a difference too. I suspect there are readers who identify with what has been written in this chapter—for those readers I trust that the examples and lessons drawn from them will serve as an inspiration, encouraging them to overcome the difficulties they have to face.

It is perfectly understandable if you have been seriously discouraged by something that went wrong, or even by a series of failures, but it is not understandable if you have decided to quit and become a bystander. For your benefit, for those you love, for your community, and even for your country, you need to start over again; learn from your experiences and put them to good effect. Become a resolute leader. Please, do try again. Go on, give it another try.

CHAPTER 7
The Exemplary Leader

....

Everyone has a reputation at his or her place of work: Jill is fun to be with; Mary is very clever; Walter has vast experience; and Phil knows all the latest information. Other colleagues attract descriptors, unspoken in their presence, that are a lot less flattering: Jack is argumentative; Al is moody; Lizzie is conceited; and Sally tries to dominate; and occasionally those sobriquets become hurtful put-downs. Once those reputations have been formed it is very difficult to change them—it might be easy in the rather superficial management films where someone is transformed overnight through a magical training intervention, but in real life altering the perception of someone's reputation is much harder to achieve.

Imagine having a reputation for being an example to others, of being a force for good, of helping to make a company an excellent place to work. Lennick and Kiel, in their book *Moral Intelligence*,[58] introduce the term *moral intelligence*, which at its simplest level means "the ability to differentiate right from wrong as defined by universal principles," and they go on to explain that "universal principles are those beliefs about human conduct that are common to all cultures around the world." As they develop their concept they make this point:

> The best leaders…are, quite simply, good people who consistently tap into their inborn disposition to be moral. They follow a moral compass—even when it's tempting not to. They make hard choices between right and wrong, or even between two different "rights."

There are leaders with a reputation for being an example to others, of being a force for good, of helping to make their company an excellent place to work. What a reputation to possess: someone who is honest, responsible, who values others and forgives, and much else. I call this the exemplary leader, and it is the type of leader you can become, if you wish. There are many ways in which to become this example to others, this exemplary leader, and in what follows I outline the main ways—there are other ways, of course, but these are among the best approaches that anyone can take. These points are aimed primarily at those performing recognised leadership roles, but it is important to emphasise that you do not need to hold a formal leadership position to exercise this form of exemplary leadership. This leadership emanates from the way in which you live your life and is called *leadership* for the simple reason that it will attract followers, people who will see your example, respect it, and want to follow it. Exemplary leadership has eight components.

1. LOVE

Love sounds like a strange word to apply to the workplace and to the leader's relationship with others, but that is because of the paucity of the English language in this particular area. In many other languages there are different words to signify the dimensions, or separate aspects, of love. One *love* word may describe feelings that pass between a man and woman when they describe themselves as "being in love," and in this sense there is an element of passion in the word; another word for love may express feelings towards members of the family and others who are close; and another *love* word could be used for the reciprocal relationship between a parent and child.

Kathleen Patterson demonstrates the potential impact of the meaning of love within the workplace:

> ...*agapao* love, or the Greek term for moral love, meaning to do the right thing at the right time and for the right reasons. *Agapao* love means to love in a social or moral sense....This type of love applies to today's leaders, in that leaders must consider the needs of their followers. This love is shown by leaders who consider each person as a total person—one with needs, wants, and desires....[59]

Therefore, demonstrating love in the workplace does not refer to sexual love or love within the natural family, and it is a rare person who has attained such a position as to be able to love everyone including those who have insulted, injured, or humiliated them. The love to consider is the love defined by Patterson—a love towards colleagues, a love that has their best interests at heart, a love that does not retaliate, a love that does not want unpleasant things to happen to those who have caused the exemplary leader harm, a love that reacts graciously when offended. It means genuinely wanting good things for other people, acting in their best interest without any sense of there being preconditions or in the hope that they will reciprocate the act. In other words, the actions of the exemplary leader are without any sense of how they will benefit from such action, how it will be to their long-term advantage.

This is not "pie in the sky" dreaming, a view of the world completely divorced from reality. Rather, it is a state of behaviour that should be everyone's goal and a conduct that the exemplary leader employs to show that love is possible, even towards those who by usual human standards do not deserve such munificence. The respected writers James Kouzes and Barry Posner show no hesitancy in advocating the necessity for the application of love in the workplace and quote numerous sources to back up their advocacy, adding these arresting words:

> Still, not a week goes by that we don't hear someone in an executive role say something to this effect: "I don't care if people like me. I just want them to respect me." Get real! This statement is utter nonsense—contrary to everything we know about effective leadership.[60]

Lance Secretan, in his book *Inspire*, makes a similar point in even more direct style:

> Where did we learn the myth that we can get our way more effectively with petulance or through aggression and violence than with love?...We know that we all yearn for more love in our lives. But we delude ourselves when we think this is only true of our personal lives and is not just as vital to our work environments.[61]

No one is suggesting for one moment that any of this is easy or, to be perfectly frank, that this level can be consistently maintained by anyone other than the most saintly of people, but the exemplary leader does his or her level best to achieve these standards and to live a life summed up in Robert Browning's words:

> Ah, but a man's reach should exceed his grasp, or what's a heaven for?[62]

Love in this context does not include any sloppy sentimentality, but a genuine commitment to having the interests of other people at heart and behaving towards them in a way that the exemplary leader would like to be treated by others.

2. JOY

This is the tale of the two people: one who was like a thermometer and one who was like a thermostat. The thermometer person would react to the prevailing environment, and if the atmosphere was cold then they would be cold; if it was warm then they would be warm, and they also knew how to become quite frosty or intemperate. The thermostat person was the complete opposite. Each day they would set the temperature at an optimal level and throughout the day would stick resolutely to their prechosen warm and sunny disposition.

It may be a simple tale, but it contains a very important truth: some people in this world allow themselves to be controlled by their circumstances. If their colleagues are gloomy then they too are gloomy; if their colleagues are full of hope and optimism, then they too show similar positive characteristics. Their dispositions appear to be controlled by external stimuli rather than by internal strengths—in other words they are thermometers rather than thermostats. Thermostat people are the complete opposite.

To speak of someone possessing joy does not mean that they go around the workplace cracking never-ending streams of jokes or that they laugh more than anyone else—that would be truly unbearable; but they are the sort of person whose disposition is not governed by outward circumstances. This does not mean that they do not cry at the death of a loved one or that they are not distressed when they observe behaviour bringing shame to the perpetrators and those associated with them. It does, however, mean that they have a joy within them produced by their ability to see a greater purpose, to understand that there is a much bigger picture, and to know that they can transcend the events taking place within their immediate proximity. The source of their joy has a far greater preeminence than the mere circumstances laid out before them, and as such the people who possess this joy are…a joy to be with: they can transform the environment of a company, they can be positive even when the going gets tough, and as a result they are most definitely an example to others. They are exemplary leaders.

3. PEACE

John Lennon may have been an unrealistic romantic dreamer, but his charge to "Give Peace a Chance" captured the thoughts and aspirations of a generation and more of people across the world. Unfortunately, peace has remained little more than a dream in the affairs of many nations and in the conduct of far too many individuals towards one another. Another singer–song writing legend, Joni Mitchell, in her "California" lyrics, captured the reality of life for many people when she lamented the fact that peace hadn't been given a chance but remained a dream for some. Yet peace remains the most alluring of goals for countries and individuals.

The word *peace* can be used in different ways when speaking of nations: for example, to describe the relationships existing among countries—being at peace with one's neighbours; or the peace that exists within a country's borders, where the rule of law is clear for everyone to see. The word *peace* can also be used to describe the state of being that exists within an individual: to be at peace with oneself and with other people—a personal peace signifying a tranquility within that helps an individual maintain serenity even when the surrounding world appears to be troubled.[a]

---

a. My etymological and historical understanding of this word, and of many of the other eight terms, is due in no small part to the writings of William Barclay—see reference section.

Many organisations and their management teams can be described in imaginative and colourful ways, but the word *peaceful* would not be one of the adjectives that springs to mind! These teams are seething hotbeds of contentious rivalry, of people who see bickering and oneupmanship as normal and expected conduct. Managers are at war with one another and make a virtue of it: they want to beat their opponents into submission and enjoy using language taken from the battlefield. The word *peace* is anathema to them, and if they did not have sufficient enemies to fight, then they would go and find some more. They pull up the drawbridges around their company and see those outside their boundary walls as existing and potential adversaries; there is nothing they like more than engaging in battle, usually through the offices of their lawyers, who can be relied upon to produce the perfect letter or statement to attack or fend off these real and/or imaginary enemies. *War, war, war* is much preferred to *jaw, jaw, jaw*, to quote Winston Churchill's famous line out of context.

To be at peace is a much better state for an individual and for a company, and the exemplary leader who is at peace can influence an organisation for good. Just imagine the impact a peaceful individual can have within a leadership team, or a project group, if they are prepared to speak up for alternative ways of seeing the world: one where peace is regarded as a virtue, one where others are seen first as potential collaborators rather than as enemies, and where true competitors are treated respectfully and carefully (recognising the realities of commercial life). People possessing this inner peace make major contributuions to their companies, and their calm dispositions are seen as produced by authority; they can be trusted to take control when their companies need such qualities, and their ability to replace volatility with tranquility is respected. They will replace suspicion of other people's motives with genuine dialogue that explores opportunities to work in harmony. Where genuine differences of opinion exist, it is far better to have the exemplary leader at the helm, someone at peace within, rather than someone whose emotional outbursts might exacerbate potential disputes.

4. PATIENCE

If most people know the saying "Patience is a virtue," then why is it relatively few make any attempt to practise this particular virtue? True patience means demonstrating long-suffering towards other people, even when the limits of patience are being tested to their limits. For the exemplary leader, this includes times when they feel they may have been wronged by the very person testing their patience, and certainly includes the concept of not taking revenge on people even when the opportunity presents itself. The exemplary leader does not become angry quickly and realises that levels of patience can be increased by recalling to mind those occasions when other people could have been impatient or angry with them. The patience they were shown may have allowed the nascent exemplary leader to develop as an individual over time.

Some people take pride in being the type of leader who "doesn't suffer fools gladly," suggesting that they are men and women of action who only work with those people who can immediately understand their point of view and make meaningful and substantial contributions to the objectives being pursued. More fool them. There are many opportunities for people of differing abilities and temperaments to make valuable contributions over time, and it makes sense to treat them patiently, seeking avenues where those talents can make meaningful offerings. The exemplary leader also sees a moral issue in this: how dare people treat others contemptibly merely because they were not able to "connect" with them immediately or because of an initial difficulty.

Admittedly, there are people in all organisations who would "test the patience of a saint," and modern businesses may not have much room for saintly practice. As a general rule, the exemplary leader does his or her best to accommodate a variety of "differently-abled" people and is reluctant to concede that there are times when someone is clearly not able to perform *any* suitable duties, no matter what training and allowances that have been given to that person. In those circumstances, and with a heavy heart, the exemplary leader believes there to be a finite point to the practice of patience.

Many successful business leaders see patience as a necessary accompaniment for medium to longer-term prosperity within the company. Many a venture has come to grief when those in charge of it were unwilling to wait for the right moment to exploit an advantage or were premature in pressing home a supposed advantage. However, some so-called business gurus suggest that impatience, rather than patience, is the virtue their disciples should pursue. In their opinion, those who pursue patience as an ideal are putting up with an unacceptable status quo, unwilling to "rattle cages" to make things happen and bring about change in their companies. Their line of argument continues: leaders who wish to create benefits from bringing change to their businesses must be impatient, especially with the stasis caused by patience, and such impatience will help bring about positive results.

Unfortunately, those holding such views completely misunderstand the true meaning of patience. There are times when actions need to be taken promptly, without undue delay, but to believe that speed of action is the antithesis of patience is quite wrong, and it is persons such as these who will often act too quickly and then repent at leisure. If only they had acquired a degree of patience along their entrepreneurial journey, if only they could see that in the medium or even longer term their ideas would have come to fruition. Unfortunately, for them it was a case that the quicker they moved the slower the company prospered; if only they had been willing to learn from those who understand that there is a proper time to act and that patience is truly a worthwhile virtue.

5. KINDNESS AND GOODNESS

These two attributes are interchangeable: kindness is closely related to goodness, which in turn is closely related to generosity. It is a case of a kindness that is good and a goodness that is kind, with both related to a generosity of spirit in dealings with others. These attributes should never be interpreted as some form of weakness, as it is possible to be kind, good, and generous and, at the same time, strong and determined.

Leadership writers James Kouzes and Barry Posner affirm this principle in discussing work colleagues who fail to deliver on commitments made:

We need to give them the same opportunities we afford ourselves to try and fail and try again. We need to give them the chance to be the best they can be. We need to support them in their growth....[63]

Similarly, Doug Lennick and Fred Kiel, in their impressive work on the concept of moral intelligence, highlight the importance of compassion and forgiveness:

Compassion is vital because caring about others not only communicates our respect for others, but creates a climate in which others will be compassionate toward us.... Forgiveness is a crucial principle, because without a tolerance for mistakes and the knowledge of our own imperfection, we are likely to be rigid, inflexible, and unable to engage with others....[64]

And Stephen Covey, in his latest book, *The 8th Habit: From Effectiveness to Greatness*, emphasises among other things the importance of forgiving other people. Commencing the "Forgiving" section of his book with the well-known Gandhi quote "Anger is an acid that can do more harm to the vessel in which it stands than to anything on which it is poured," Covey goes on to advocate a forgiving attitude to those who have done us wrong, often inadvertently or through carelessness, and discusses the experience of two people who had been hurt:

More negative energy was released until they were extremely open to the whole idea that no one can do us any harm without our consent and that our chosen response is the key determiner of our life—that we are a product of our decisions, not our conditions.[65]

Covey places his finger on the principle that in being angry with others and harbouring bitterness against them deep within, individuals do more harm to themselves than they do to other people.

It is harder to be kind, good, and generous in the workplace than to be nasty, bad tempered, and mean-spirited. Some of the latter type of managers—bad tempered, taking advantage of someone's error, and lacking any sense of graciousness in their dealings with people—appear to succeed in the short term and in the longer term also. Often people look up to them, hailing them as good examples of achieving managers, but working with such people is an unpleasant experience for most of their colleagues. Over time, many of them (but not all of them, unfortunately) are forced out of the company when the substantial downside of their mean-spiritedness is discovered. In the longer run, their bosses realise that their style of management is doing more harm than good to the company.

One author[66] wrote about a management type termed the *veni, vidi, vanished* category. People of this management style come into the company amidst a fanfare announcing their arrival; they proclaim loudly, to whoever will listen, what they will achieve (while at the same time lamenting the parlous state of affairs they have discovered within the organisation, thereby criticising their predecessors). Within a relatively short period of time, they leave the company, claiming to be moving on to their next management challenge, but everyone knows that the reason for the change of direction is that they haven't lived up to their boasts. The converse to this type is the quietly stated yet highly successful manager that Jim Collins[67] describes (and I refer to in chapter 3). As one reads Collins's analytical description of these successful leaders, it suggests that some of the principal reasons for their success are their essential kindness, goodness, and generosity of spirit. One way to demonstrate generosity of spirit is to give time and commitment to helping others in practical ways, such as through mentoring or by being available to sit and listen and offer advice.

These words from John Wesley[68] sum up perfectly the application of kindness and goodness:

> Do all the good you can,
> By all the means you can,
> In all the ways you can,
> In all the places you can,

At all the times you can,
To all the people you can,
As long as ever you can.

6. FAITHFULNESS

The exemplary leader places a high value on faithfulness and does his or her best to practise it: personally, by remaining true to inner convictions and principles; collegially, by being dependable to coworkers; and corporately, through a commitment to the aims and objectives of the organisation. Faithfulness is never seen as some far-off aim, as if it was a Utopian dream, but is seen as something tangible and practical. It is the quality of a man or woman who is known to be reliable; who will not let someone down when a situation depends on them and the circumstances within their control.

In all walks of life, people value faithfulness and hold up for admiration those colleagues, friends, and family who will never let another person down. Faithfulness is such an admired and desired quality that over the years songwriters have sentimentalised it.[69] Many will remember cowboys' songs about the faithfulness of their "four-legged friends" (horses). On a far more important level, songwriters have properly spiritualised faithfulness as a key attribute of God: *Great is Thy faithfulness, O God my Father; There is no shadow of turning with Thee.*[70] Unquestionably, people want to believe in a God on whom they can rely; someone in whom they can invest their trust and hope; and someone who will be faithful, especially in times of trial. This divine faithfulness is of a different order to human faithfulness, but the principle remains the same: people want colleagues and leaders who can be trusted and relied upon. And they want that faithfulness to be reflected in their own lives too, as this quote from Mother Teresa illustrates: "I do not pray for success, I ask for faithfulness."

People value the person who can be depended upon, where they know their friendship will not be governed by some selfish consideration, such as what benefit can be gained from the relationship. Conversely, it is considered abominable to encounter those who can best be described as life's chameleons: they totally support a person, they are there at their right hand, right up until there comes a moment when they discover that their career opportunities can be better advanced by abandoning the person and expressing views opposite to what they once believed, or at least opposite to what they once said.

Exemplary leaders understand that faithfulness is a valuable commodity, at all levels and in all relationships, and make it their aim to be faithful to those they consider to be a part of their community of contacts. At times this can be difficult and may even involve conflicting challenges and difficult conversations with friends and family when behaviour or attitudes are questionable, but when those difficulties are overcome, faithfulness is treasured as a precious commodity by all concerned. In terms of the workplace, such faithfulness involves: being the type of person that others can depend on; having a reputation for reliability; being trusted to retain the personal and confidential information that someone has entrusted to you; sticking with people through "thick and thin," especially when they are going through difficult times; and being loyal to the company's aims and objectives.

7. GENTLENESS

Gentleness sounds like a strange concept to consider in today's world of business. Surely, business demands cutthroat practices where it's "dog eat dog," and gentleness would be one of the very last qualities someone needed, unless they wished to be trampled to death in the rush of competitors trying to take advantage of their perceived supine position. In terms of business practice, most people would interpret the word *gentleness* perjoratively and consider it to be an unsuitable, even unthinkable, concept for the twenty-first-century world of work. Only the most open-minded would be prepared to sit back and consider whether it was really possible to be gentle in one's dealings with another person. Most would dismiss it as a really unsuitable and irrelevant concept.

The proper and full meaning of the word *gentleness* signals a number of interrelated concepts:

It has three main meanings. (a) It means being submis-
sive…(b) It means being teachable, being not too proud
to learn…(c) Most often of all it means being considerate….[71]

or

Equitable, fair, moderate…not insisting on the letter of
the law; it expresses that considerateness that looks
humanely and reasonably at the facts of a case.[72]

No wonder it is a word open to misinterpretation; the proper
and full meaning of the word runs counter to the wimpishness suggested in most people's minds when they hear of someone being
described as gentle. The correct use of the word makes it a wonderful word for use in the business world, and such an inviting challenge. There are aspects of the definition that may well be
inappropriate—for example, practising submissiveness at the wrong
moments may be inviting trouble—but there are other aspects of the
definition that can make it a highly appropriate term for exemplary
leadership practice. For one thing, it means the complete opposite of
being contentious, and that must be a good thing. Everyone knows
people who are contentious—they could start an argument in an
empty room, as the saying goes. Whatever is said to them, they want
to espouse the opposite point of view. That is the way some people
have been trained to think—by putting up the counterargument, by
"mismatching" as some analysts refer to it. Others, however, just love
the prospect of a good fight, and what a draining experience it can be
to sit in their presence for more than a few hours.

The word *gentleness* also conjures up thoughts of being teachable, of being able and willing to learn, rather than being the sort of
person who conveys the impression of being a know-it-all. And then
there is the notion of being humble—some of the most impressive
people are also among the most humble. And, the word *gentleness*
means being considerate of others. Magnificent!—that is what is
needed, to be an exemplary leader considerate of the needs of other
people. Then, the word contains the idea of being the sort of person

who can look objectively and rationally at the facts of a case and arrive calmly at a conclusion.

The word *gentle* also conjures up thoughts that are the very opposite of being brash and abrasive in relationships with other people. Gentleness does not suggest any weakness of character or personality flaw that can be exploited by business competitors. It signifies an inner strength that enables the exemplary leader to arrive at properly considered decisions, to tackle big and difficult issues, and to do it in a manner that respects the position of other people and recognises the limitations and human weaknesses of the person making the decision. A gentle person is a balanced, well-rounded individual, and the concept of gentleness is central to the make-up of the exemplary leader.

8. SELF-CONTROL

One of the most unpleasant things to observe in any company are leaders who cannot control themselves. They are subject to rants and raves, lose control of their tempers, make injudicious decisions, and lose the respect of the people they have been asked to lead. They would do well to consider these words from Doug Lennick and Fred Kiel:

> Effective leaders rely on self-control to maintain alignment with principles. Most leaders know that losing emotional control is bad for their self-esteem, their reputations, and their business performance.[73]

Self-control runs counter to the way many people run their lives: some people are damaging the very fabric of their environment through a lack of control of their resources; some are damaging their health through other lack of control; "Doin' your own thing" has given some licence to behave selfishly and unacceptably towards others; and those who suggest that there is merit in exercising certain disciplines in the way people should live their lives are laughed at for being old-fashioned fuddy-duddies. As a result, many people who are seen as traditional in their views are left wondering whether it is just plain old-fashioned to understand one's weaknesses and to keep them in check. In other words, is it out of step with the modern world to preach the merits of personal self-control?

Self-control is a key component in how lives should be lived. It is through self-control (or self-discipline, willpower, restraint, or strength of mind) that you can be the sort of person who is seen to practice love, to be joyful, to exude peace and patience, to be kind and good, to be known for your faithfulness, and to be gentle—and all of those terms are used in the context of the way they have been defined in this chapter. Conversely, where self-control is missing, leaders are likely to be self-indulgent and unproductive in their dealings with other people. That may be a hard message to swallow, but it is central to, and a logical conclusion of, the very challenge of this chapter. I would also contend that the evidence people see around them every day of their working lives, where they are unfortunate enough to be led by those who lack self-control, backs up my contention.

Emphasising the benefits of self-control risks sounding like someone who enjoys spoiling the party, but actually the very opposite is true. Enjoying the journey that lies ahead depends on the degree of self-control exercised. Just think of the athlete who wins Olympic gold: suddenly, all those early morning exercise sessions, the strict diet, the parties that had to be missed, are as nothing compared with the sheer joy of standing on the podium and listening to their national anthem being played. No one would suggest, for one moment, that exemplary leaders will experience the exhilarating thrill of a Carl Lewis or Usain Bolt when they exercise self-control in the workplace—that would be ridiculous. There is, however, a satisfaction when actions are undertaken honourably, when other people have been treated properly, and when the exemplary leader maintains control of the way he or she conducted business.

Conclusion

To be an exemplary leader takes courage and inner strength that can only come from deeply held beliefs and values. It is rare for individuals to say one thing, in terms of their moral or ethical position, and then to do the complete opposite—although there are exceptions to that general rule. For most people it takes a gradual slide away from their guiding morals or ethics: they start gradually, almost imperceptibly, then they drift, and over a period of time they arrive at a place that is some distance away from where they first started. Often they do not realise that they have travelled any distance at all.

That is why it is essential for the person who wants to be an exemplary leader to take regular checks, an audit, of where he or she stands as an individual. Otherwise it is quite astonishing how this imperceptible slide can take place in an individual, even in an experienced person, and when this slide happens there will be people who will find pleasure in taking the opportunity to call the exemplary leader a hypocrite. The worst thing for an exemplary leader to hear are the words: "Come down off your high horse—you're just the same as us." That hurts and can be a terminable experience, meaning the end of the line for any attempt to make a real difference within an organisation. Finding time to conduct a self-audit also reduces the likelihood that a belief in principles has actually turned over time into unattractive self-righteousness and priggishness—the very last qualities to possess.

In addition to taking stock of things, the wise exemplary leader will also have a simple but trusted framework against which all actions can be tested. Many have found the following set of words to be extremely helpful. They are not a set of rules in the conventional sense of that phrase, nor are they a typical set of values, but they do represent a guide that challenges an individual to consider whether their principles and practices are being maintained at a high standard.

> Finally…whatever is true, whatever is honourable, whatever is just, whatever is pure, whatever is pleasing, whatever is commendable, if there is any excellence and if there is anything worthy of praise, think about these things. [74]

Summary—The Exemplary Leader Possesses:

1. Love
2. Joy
3. Peace
4. Patience
5. Kindness and goodness
6. Faithfulness
7. Gentleness
8. Self-control

PART 3

CONCLUSION

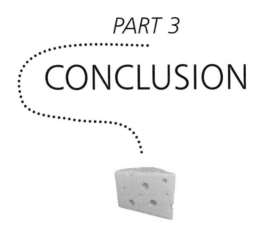

CHAPTER 8
You Can Move the Cheese!

··

This final chapter contains a profound personal challenge: it invites you to believe that you can help *move the cheese* and then act on the basis of that belief. If you respond positively to the challenge, the consequences are likely to change your life and the lives of others. Before presenting this challenge in more detail I need to recapitulate on some of the key points made so far.

We live in a world that is changing rapidly and dealing with the different components of change, the positive and the negative aspects, has become a common feature in the lives of most people. This book has limited itself to the changes taking place within the organisation (private, public, and not-for-profit) and the possibilities offered by those changes to make a positive difference in the lives of people.

Spencer Johnson's popular and helpful book *Who Moved My Cheese?*[75] uses the metaphor of cheese to represent those various changes and amusingly explains how four characters (one might say four different personality types) react to the need to search for new cheese when their current stock runs out. The story perceptively describes the challenges people encounter in dealing with change and the pursuit of their hopes and aspirations—in other words, in search of their cheese. One of Johnson's many telling points exclaims, "We keep doing the same things over and over again and wonder why things don't get better...," and his thought encourages everyone dealing with change to ask: Do I keep doing the same things over and over again, making the same mistakes, pretending that things will be different the next time? Do I assume that the mere act of being active will result in meaningful differences, or do I really take advantage of the opportunities presented by change to make a positive difference, to actually improve the way things are done in my organisation? They may be two long-winded questions, but they are of cardinal importance.

There are possibilities to be explored, opportunities to be discovered, and longer-term goals to be realised in the search for new cheese that will satisfy. For some it will be a relatively straightforward journey: they work for organisations that provide substantial encouragement; it is crystal clear that they believe in people, want the very best for their people, and believe that by focusing on the contribution of their people they will build the company further. For others it will be arduous and challenging: they work in organisations where the prospect of introducing significant changes in the way people are treated is daunting. Whether substantial and large or gradual and small, there can be tangible *moving the cheese* benefits for all, and these improvements must be celebrated and never ignored.

Irrespective of the type of organisation and the degree of change, the challenges facing those committed to *moving the cheese* will have many similar characteristics, as Johnson acknowledges: "Whatever parts of us we choose to use, we all share something in common: a need to find our way in the maze and succeed in changing times." For this reason, above all others, the title of my book became *You Can Move the Cheese!* as it encourages you to see and to believe that you can make a difference to the lives of others by the way in which you view them and behave towards them; by the way in which your leadership style and practice makes new cheese available to all.

How can you do this? How can you bring about change? How can you help *move the cheese* for others? How can you find a way through the maze of organisational life? This is the profound personal challenge I spoke of earlier, and it involves becoming a purposeful, principled, resourceful, and exemplary leader. These four dimensions of leadership, based on fundamental and long-standing personal principles that have stood the test of time, will influence the way in which you act, enabling you to become the leader you ought to be and, over time, will bring about change (new cheese) in your sphere of influence.

It may be that your contribution will be large and visible for all to see, or it may be that you have a small and humble contribution to make and there will never be a plaque on the wall to commemorate what you contributed. After all, few people are destined to become a president or prime minister, an international sports or film star, win a Nobel Prize for their work, invent something that will be hailed as a major discovery, or even become the CEO of the company. That does not matter because whatever you contribute in a meaningful way to make things better for other people has an intrinsic worth all of its own. Whether your contribution is small or large, you have helped make the world of work a better place for others and yourself.

Eleanor Roosevelt, the First Lady of the United States from 1933 to 1945, is often credited with having coined the phrase, "It's better to light a candle than curse the darkness," although, in truth, the phrase probably found fame when used by Adlai Stevenson speaking in praise of Eleanor Roosevelt in a 1962 United Nations General Assembly address, when he said: "She would rather light candles than curse the darkness, and her glow has warmed the world." I want to suggest that the opportunities and challenges being presented are best summed up in the picture of a single candle. Many of you might say that there is no real possibility of transforming your companies, of creating the opportunity for people to flourish—to show their true worth and to feel that they are making valuable contributions, to experience personal fulfilment and to benefit the organisation. I say it *is* possible to make a difference: if only enough people were determined to behave differently and to lead their people according to the principles set out here, then there would be a transformation in the lives of many.

The challenge of this book is to encourage you to become the person who is willing to go about your place of work lighting candles…metaphorical candles, of course. Some of you might be able only to light one small candle, a candle the size of the one sitting proudly on top of a birthday cake; it might seem small and puny, an insignificant candle, but enough of those candles bring considerable illumination. Other people may be able to light big candles, the sort of candle used in cathedrals; candles that send out large amounts of light. Imagine what would happen if thousands of those candles were lit across the country: the light would be visible to many. Almost certainly, your actions will not bring you the fame of Eleanor Roosevelt, but in your place of work you could help transform the very nature of people's experience and make a small but important contribution to liberating the talents of fellow countrymen and women.

From one famous woman to another: George Eliot wrote, "It's never too late to be who you might have been." Do you believe those words, or do you consider them a trifle idealistic and unrealistic? Do you think you have gone beyond the point of no return and that there are genuine valid reasons why you can't be *who you might have been*—reasons of family upbringing, or personal reputation, or managerial track record, or whatever other reasons come to mind as you ponder Eliot's words? Perhaps you have become stuck in your ways and see the possibility of change as most unwelcome, or there may be other reasons that justify your decision for inaction, but I want to encourage you to believe that it is not too late, no matter what your background and no matter what seemingly unassailable obstacles stand in your path. Eliot's words are inspirational, and whatever your circumstances, let me encourage you one more time: you can help to *move the cheese.*

That then is the challenge: to become a purposeful, principled, resourceful, and exemplary leader. To become the sort of person who serves a greater and higher purpose, who lives and leads by deeply held principles, who acts effectively in their company, who influences things for good, who may work silently and without visible praise but who gets the right things done.

You can make a difference in your place of work.

YOU CAN MOVE THE CHEESE!

This is the true joy in life, being used for a purpose recognized by yourself as a mighty one. Being a force of nature instead of a feverish, selfish little clod of ailments and grievances complaining that the world will not devote itself to making you happy. I am of the opinion that my life belongs to the whole community and as I live it is my privilege—my "privilege" to do for it whatever I can. I want to be thoroughly used up when I die, for the harder I work the more I love. I rejoice in life for its own sake. Life is no brief candle to me; it is a sort of splendid torch which I've got a hold of for the moment and I want to make it burn as brightly as possible before handing it on to future generations.

—George Bernard Shaw[76]

References

Preface

1. Spencer Johnson, *Who Moved My Cheese?* (London: Vermillion, 1998).

Chapter 1

2. Thomas E. Rick, *Fiasco: The American Military Adventure in Iraq* (London: Penguin Books, 2006).

Chapter 3

3. Toby Moore, *The Times*, 23.08.06.
4. Harry Mount, *The Daily Telegraph*, 21.08.06.
5. Alan Hamilton, *The Times*, 23.08.06.
6. Anushka Asthana, *The Observer*, 27.08.06.
7. The Chartered Institute of Personnel Development (CIPD) research is based on the following sources: CIPD, *Absence Management Survey Report* (London: CIPD, 2006); R. Wheatley, *Taking the Strain: A Survey of Managers and Workplace Stress* (London: Institute of Management, 2000); N. Doherty and S. Tyson, *Mental Well-Being in the Workplace: A Resource Pack for Management Training and Development* (Sudbury, UK: HSE Books, 1998); HSE, *Work-Related Stress Information Pack* (Sudbury, UK: HSE Books, 2000); A. Smith, S. Johal, and E. Wadsworth, *The Scale of Occupational Stress: The Bristol Stress and Health at Work Study* (Sudbury, UK: HSE Books, 2000).

8. Marcus Buckingham and Donald O. Clifton, *Now, Discover Your Strengths: How to Develop Your Talents and Those of the People You Manage* (London: Simon & Schuster UK Ltd., 2002).

9. Stephen R. Covey, *The 8th Habit: From Effectiveness to Greatness* (London: Simon & Schuster UK Ltd., 2004).

10. Chartered Institute of Personnel Management (CIPD), Factsheet 151, The Broadway, London SW19 1JQ. CIPD annual survey report, 2006.

11. T. A. Stewart, *Intellectual Capital* (London: Nicholas Brealey Publishing Limited, 1998).

12. Quoted in Chris Lee and Ron Zemke, "The Search for Spirit in the Workplace," in Larry C. Spears, ed., *Reflections on Leadership* (New York: John Wiley and Sons, 1995).

13. Jim Collins, *Good to Great* (London: Random House Business Books, 2001).

14. Bill George, *Authentic Leadership* (San Francisco: Jossey-Bass, 2003).

15. Peter Block, *Stewardship* (San Francisco: Berret-Koehler Publishers, 1996).

16. Ken Blanchard, *Managing by Values* (San Francisco: Berret-Koehler Publishers, 1997).

17. Danah Zohar and Ian Marshall, *Spiritual Capital* (London: Bloomsbury Publishing Plc, 2004).

18. Robert K. Greenleaf, *The Servant as Leader* (available from the Greenleaf Center for Servant Leadership, Indianapolis).

19. Stephen Prosser, *To Be a Servant-Leader* (New York/ Mahwah, NJ: Paulist Press, 2007).

Chapter 4

20. Ephesians 4:1.

21. Ephesians 4:25–32; Colossians 3:7–9, 4:1; 1 Peter 2:1–3; 1 Thessalonians 4:11–12; James 1:19–27; 1 Peter 3:8–16.

22. Acts 9:1–31, 10:1–48; James 2:1–9; Philippians 2:14–15; Romans 14:1–23, 15:1–7.

23. Hebrews 5:11–14; 2 Peter 1:5–8.

24. Matthew 20:20–38; Mark 10:35–45; Romans 12:1–8; Philippians 2:3–4.

25. Ephesians 6:5–9; Hebrews 12:7–13; 2 Thessalonians 3:6–14; John 6:60–71.

26. 1 Peter 5:7.

27. Manfred Kets de Vries, *The Leader on the Couch—A Clinical Approach to Changing People and Organizations* (Chichester, England: John Wiley & Sons, and San Francisco: Jossey-Bass, 2006).

28. Matthew 5:13–16. (I am indebted to William Barclay's commentary on Matthew's Gospel for the ideas contained in the two paragraphs on salt and light, and for the historical context.)

29. Matthew 5:41 (with acknowledgements to William Barclay).

30. Charles Handy, *Age of Unreason: New Thinking for a New World* (London: Random House, 2002).

31. Matthew 5:38–47, 7:1–6, 18:15–17.

32. Acts 15:36–41; 1 Corinthians 1:10–17; Galatians 1:11–21; 2 Timothy 2:23–26; James 3:3–18; 3 John 9—10; Jude 4—16; Ephesians 4:1–16.

33. Romans 12:4–8; 1 Corinthians 12:1–31.

34. 2 Corinthians 8:1–15, 9:6–15; Ephesians 6:1–10.

35. Matthew 13:53–58, 26:31–35; Mark 6:1–6, 14:60–72; John 4:43–54, 13:31–38; Acts 16:16.

Chapter 5

36. Rosabeth Moss Kanter, *On the Frontiers of Management* (Boston: Harvard Business School Publishing, 2004).

37. Matthew 7:24–27; Luke 6:46–49.

38. Matthew 13:1–23; Mark 4:1–20; Luke 18:1–15.

39. Matthew 13:31–35, 44–46; Mark 4:30–34; Luke 13:18–21.

40. Luke 11:5–8.

41. Matthew 25:14–30; Luke 12:42–48, 19:11–27.

42. Matthew 18:10–14; Luke 15:1–32.

43. Philip Yancy, *What's So Amazing About Grace?* (Grand Rapids, MI: Zondervan, 1997).

44. Michael Green, *The Message of Matthew*, Bible Speaks Today Series (Leicester, England: Inter-Varsity Press, 1988).

45. Matthew 18:21–35; Luke 7:41–43.
46. Matthew 20:1–16.
47. Matthew 21:28–32.
48. Mark 4:26–29.
49. Luke 10:25–37.
50. Luke 12:13–21, 16:19–31, 18:9–14, 20:9–19; Matthew 21:33–46; Mark 12:1–12.
51. Luke 18:1–18.
52. Matthew 24:32–35; Mark 13:28–31; Luke 21:29–31.
53. Stephen Prosser, *To Be a Servant-Leader* (New York/ Mahwah, NJ: Paulist Press, 2007).
54. Luke 17:7–10.
55. Matthew 9:16–17; Mark 2:21–22; Luke 5:36–39.

Chapter 6

56. Luke 22:32–34, 54–62 (NIV UK).
57. © Chris Skellern, AIE. Source: www.aie.org.uk 2001.

Chapter 7

58. Doug Lennick and Fred Kiel, *Moral Intelligence* (Upper Saddle River, NJ: Pearson Education, 2005).
59. Kathleen Patterson, "Servant Leadership: A Theoretical Model" (Regent University, Virginia Beach, VA: Servant Leadership Round Table, 2003).
60. James M. Kouzes and Barry Z. Posner, *A Leader's Legacy* (San Francisco: Jossey-Bass, 2006).
61. Lance Secretan, *Inspire* (Hoboken, NJ: John Wiley & Sons, 2004).
62. Robert Browning, English poet 1812–89. To be found in various compilations.
63. James M. Kouzes and Barry Z. Posner, *A Leader's Legacy* (San Francisco: Jossey-Bass, 2006).
64. Doug Lennick and Fred Kiel, *Moral Intelligence* (Upper Saddle River, NJ: Pearson Education, 2005).

65. Stephen R Covey, *The 8th Habit: From Effectiveness to Greatness* (London: Simon & Schuster UK Ltd., 2004).

66. Stephen Prosser, *Effective People: Leadership and Organization Development in Healthcare* (Oxford: Radcliffe Publishing, 2005).

67. Jim Collins, *Good to Great* (London: Random House Business Books, 2001).

68. Well-known John Wesley quotation.

69. "A Four Legged Friend," from the film *Son of Paleface*, lyrics by Jack Brooks, 1952. (Roy Rogers, 1952; Bob Hope & Jimmy Wakely, 1952; Andy Mackay, 1974).

70. © 1923 Hope Publishing Company, 380 South Main Place, Carol Stream, IL 60188 (800-323-1049).

71. William Barclay, *The Gospel of Matthew*, The Daily Study Bible Series (Edinburgh: Saint Andrew Press, 1986).

72. W. E. Vine, *Expository Dictionary of New Testament Words* (London: Oliphants, 1969).

73. Doug Lennick and Fred Kiel, *Moral Intelligence* (Upper Saddle River, NJ: Pearson Education, 2005).

74. Philippians 4:8.

Chapter 8

75. Spencer Johnson, *Who Moved My Cheese?* (London: Vermillion, 1998).

76. George Bernard Shaw, *Man and Superman: A Comedy and a Philosophy* (London: Penguin Fiction, 1946).

TO BE A SERVANT-LEADER

Stephen Prosser

Based upon or inspired by biblical texts, *To Be a Servant-Leader* examines the main characteristics or principles of leadership.

978-0-8091-4467-9

SERVANT LEADERSHIP MODELS FOR YOUR PARISH

Dan R. Ebener

Servant Leadership Models for Your Parish explores the practice of servant leadership in a church context. It presents seven behaviors practiced by leaders and members in high-performing parishes and provides real-life examples of these practices.

978-0-8091-4653-6

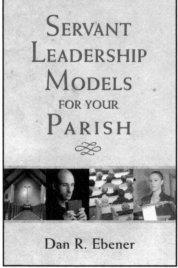

❖

SEVEN PILLARS OF SERVANT LEADERSHIP
Practicing the Wisdom of Leading by Serving
James W. Sipe and Don M. Frick

Offers a skills-oriented approach to acquiring the most critical competencies of effective Servant Leadership, all without overlooking matters of the heart and soul that make it all worthwhile.

978-0-8091-4560-7

❖

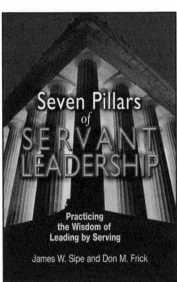

SERVANT LEADERSHIP
[25th Anniversary Edition]
A Journey into the Nature of
Legitimate Power and Greatness
Robert K. Greenleaf

A classic work on leadership for business
men and women, government leaders and
all persons in positions of authority.

0-8091-0554-3

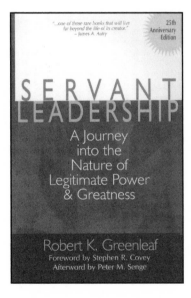

THE SERVANT-LEADER WITHIN

A Transformative Path
*Robert K. Greenleaf; edited by Hamilton Beazley,
Julie Beggs, and Larry C. Spears*

Combines in one volume classic works on
servant leadership and its relationship to the art
of teaching and the act of learning.

0-8091-4219-8

THE EMERGING DIACONATE
Servant Leaders in a Servant Church
William T. Ditewig

Sketches the current state of the permanent diaconate,
especially in the United States, then offers the historical
developments which led to the contemporary diaconate,
and finally suggests a vision of the diaconate for the
future, always within the matrix of a servant-ecclesiology
which should characterize the entire Church.

978-0-8091-4449-5

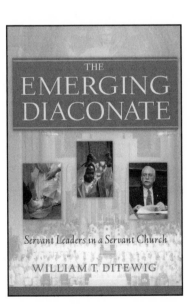

❖⦂⦂❖

A SERVANT LEADER'S JOURNEY
Lessons from Life
Jim Boyd

A series of reflections on coping with a fatal disease,
but also an insightful examination of living and
dying by a widely acclaimed authority on
organizational leadership.

978-0-8091-4568-3

❖⦂⦂❖